Rescuing Revelation

A Fresh Perspective on an Ancient Vision

Monty C. Wright

Sermon To Book
www.sermontobook.com

Rescuing Revelation / Monty C. Wright
ISBN-13: 978-1-945793-36-3
ISBN-10: 1-945793-36-8

To Emma and Liam...

Two hearts that keep mine beating.
Two lives that inspire me.
Two gifts that I couldn't live without.
May you both enjoy the mystery of God and the
pursuit of all that is seen and unseen, known and
unknown.

~Dad

Acknowledgments

The journey of creating this book was one of community, fear, study, unknowing, and shared discovery.

There are so many nuances from so many people in the pages of this book. I would like to say thank you to my staff team at Snoqualmie Valley Alliance, especially pastors Marty Benedict and Kristin Moomaw who spoke into this book and added their thoughts.

To Caleb and the editing team at Sermon to Book, thank you for your patience and desire to see this project come alive.

To the Apostle John, may we all have his ability through Christ to see what surrounds and holds us and continues to draw us toward all that is good, beautiful, and true!

~Monty

CONTENTS

Note from the Author

Thank you for purchasing *Rescuing Revelation.* This book is meant to offer real substance and context to discussions of the book of Revelation—to rescue the last book of the Bible from popular culture and bring it back to Jesus.

As a practical tool to help you get the most out of your reading, a brief set of reflective questions and a brief, action-oriented summary accompanies each chapter of the book. I recommend going through these sections with a pen and writing your thoughts in the areas provided. You can contemplate these questions by yourself, with a friend, or with a study group.

Whichever way you choose to approach this book and the workbook questions, I hope you enjoy the experience. And most of all, I pray you grow in your understanding of your identity in Christ—and of what He has in store for you.

INTRODUCTION

Approaching Revelation

There seems to be an increasing interest in things to come. Books and movies about Revelation, the apocalypse, the end times, and how the world will or might come to an end are prolific. Though rarely accurate, they reflect an undeniable curiosity about what is ahead for the world. Even if someone produces a poorly-created theological movie on what they think the end is about, I tend to love it not for its cinematic creativity and brilliance, but because it creates conversation.

Most people, not just creative book and movie screenplay writers, have experienced a divine rattling that whispers, "There is something more." They may ask themselves, "Is there something beyond this life?" or "Is there a point to this life?" It is a divine longing of the human soul, and not without reason.

Pause for a moment. Close your eyes, and think of the New Testament letter of Revelation. What comes to your mind? What images slip through your thoughts? I tend to gravitate toward themes of end-times prophecy, Armageddon, the final battle, the final victory of God, heaven, and God's majestic throne.

Traditionally, artists' renditions of Revelation have not been those of beauty or peace. More often, their pictures reflect gruesome, dark images that evoke terror or fear—the beast with the horns, a dragon with seven heads, or people surrounded by fire and writhing in misery as the wrath of God pours out of the sky like molten lava. Some think of Revelation like Frans Floris' painting from 1554, *The Fall of the Rebellious Angels*. It depicts the archangel Michael and his fighting angels battling frightening, devil-faced beasts. Others think of Revelation and recall elaborately detailed chronological charts hanging in Sunday school classrooms or old Bible study lessons.

Revelation, however, was not written to provoke fear, confusion, or division as many believe. Rather, John the Apostle, wrote down the visions he saw and the things he heard to inspire hope in early believers within seven churches experiencing the crushing persecution of the Roman Empire.

Revealing the Background of the Revelation

The title of the book of Revelation comes from the Greek word *apokalypsis*. Its actual title reads *The Apocalypse of Jesus Christ*.[1] The Greek word *apokalypsis* is a conjunction of two words: *apo* (from) and *kalypsis* (covering).[2] The revelation is thus the removal of the covering—that is, the unveiling—of Jesus Christ.

Its author, John, was the last of the original twelve apostles still living. The Roman Empire had laid a heavy boot on the throat of the known world, capturing and subduing everything in its tracks. Rome was the most powerful economic, cultural, political, and military force at that time, and everyone knew it.

In AD 70, Titus utterly destroyed Jerusalem. He ruled until AD 81 when the world experienced arguably the wickedest emperor in history, Domitian. Most have heard of the emperor Nero; his name conjures violent and psychotic images. However, Domitian gave Nero a run for his money in the area of wickedness. Domitian followed suit with his predecessor, establishing and enforcing emperor worship.[3] Emperor worship declared Caesar was a god, and therefore, all citizens were required to worship Caesar as Lord and god.[4]

For most people in the Roman Empire, that was no problem. They had a different god for every day of their lives. But for the Jew and for the Christian, this posed a great problem. There was only One whom they would bow down to and call Lord and God, the one true God of the Scriptures, and this was definitely not any emperor. Because of their refusal to worship Caesar, Christians were persecuted, abused, murdered, thrown to the lions for sport, and displayed for entertainment in the great Roman circuses. The church had nowhere to go because it wouldn't bow to Caesar, the god of the surrounding culture.

Rome still considered John a threat even in his old age. He'd been imprisoned, dipped in boiling oil, and maimed for life, but he was still alive in spite of it all.[5] Fearing John's power, the Romans exiled him to the island of Patmos. This is where John received his revelation.

A Basis for Understanding the Revelation

The Bible as a whole contains history, poetry, epistles, and prophecy. The book of Revelation possesses all of these literary characteristics. It's important to recognize this; reading the book of Revelation through only one of those lenses will result in an incorrect interpretation of the entire letter.

- **The poetic aspect** reveals the truth, reality, and beauty of God, expressed through verbal imagery in a way the reader can see, feel, hear, and taste—just as John did.
- **The prophetic aspect** exists to warn readers of the implications of a life lived apart from God.
- **The epistle aspect** serves as a pastoral reminder to encourage anyone reading the letter to have hope and faith in God and His plan of redemption.
- **Apocalyptic literature** employs the use of symbols and imagery in both literal and non-literal ways to illustrate tangible truth.

Attempting to interpret Revelation within a modern western context rather than the cultural, racial, and biblical context it was originally written in will lead to misinterpretation. Revelation was written two thousand years ago to churches who understood the letter without study groups and concordances.

There are numerous images and abundant symbolism in this book that would have been perfectly clear to first-century readers. For example, the Old Testament mentions "horns" often which were symbolic for a king or a kingdom. Understanding this, it is clear John was not referring to literal animal horns in his letter. Applying modern-day literal definitions to words and images presented in Revelation may lead to a misunderstanding of the author's original intent.

John frequently used numbers in his book, predominantly the number seven. For example, he mentions seven churches, trumpets, plagues, seals, spirits, and blessings. He also mentions seven lampstands, stars, thunders, heads of the beast, kings, horns of the Lamb, and eyes of the Lamb. In Scripture, the number seven stands for perfection and completeness.[6]

Another number mentioned often is the number six. Six is man's number, an imperfect number that is one less than seven (less than perfection).[7] Man was created on the sixth day, told to work for six days, and so on. With that in mind, recognize the number 6-6-6 shows the complete abandonment of perfection.

Remember, the original readers of John's letter knew all this already! Therefore, commit to an honest examination of the book. Read through it slowly, and let the letter unveil itself and communicate the plain meaning of the text. Reading it any other way will hijack the intended meaning and terrorize readers in ways John never intended.

Four Predominant Views

There are four major ways readers tend to view Revelation, each of which offers some value of insight.[8]

The Futurist View

This view sees the Revelation as a forecast of a future yet to unfold. The futurist holds that the majority of the prophecies in Revelation will be fulfilled in a literal way sometime in the future. In this understanding, the book unfolds chronologically through the seals, trumpets, bowls, and other images.

This is the view in the popular *Left Behind* series, which aligns well with the Premillennial-Dispensational theory. While futurists hold chapters one to three to be historically rooted in the past, everything from chapter four on is believed to be in the future.

The Preterist View

Those who hold the preterist view see the Revelation as having been completely fulfilled within the first century of the church (there are full preterists and partial preterists, but on the whole, both see Revelation as history and not a future reality). Therefore, the book is seen as symbolic images of actual first-century events. This would mean nothing written would occur in the future. All prophecies have already been fulfilled. Because of this, preterists believe there is little to ascertain from the book other than the importance of holy living and patience while waiting for Jesus to come back for His bride, the church.

The Historicist View

The historicist sees John's Revelation as something currently being fulfilled, particularly in western history as time continues while waiting for the second coming of Jesus Christ. Historicists believe the events of Revelation started in the first century and continue to this day. The images and symbols of Revelation are generally given a metaphorical definition; for example, they interpret the seven churches to represent the seven "church ages" in history.

This group ties in many current contexts and imagery and sees the prophecies of Revelation as literal historical events.

The Idealist View

Idealists see this book as an allegory of the cosmic battle between good and evil. Some idealists assume the battle between God and Satan—good and evil—is a battle between two equals. God's sovereignty, including over what Satan is permitted to do, is deemphasized or denied.

For the idealist, the events of Revelation are not connected to real historical events. Rather, they are used to explain the human struggle in life and God's ultimate victory.

Millennial Reign

Another frequent topic of debate among those who read Revelation is the use of the term "millennial." Millennial means, "one thousand." The Bible states that one day for people is like one thousand for the Lord (2 Peter 3:8). Questions regarding the millennial reign of Christ include: When will it happen? Is it a literal millennium or symbolic? What will precede the millennial reign of Christ? Is this present day a symbolic millennial reign?

These questions have divided churches for years. While I will go into more detail in Chapter 24, the following is a thumbnail view of the main millennial views:

- **The pre-millennial view** says Jesus will return to earth before He establishes His literal thousand-year reign on earth. During the millennial reign of Christ, the church—the bride of Christ—will rule and reign with Jesus over the earth from Jerusalem. In this view, Israel will finally receive the land promised to her per God's covenant. Within premillennialism, the dispensational view believes there will be a seven-year period on earth where the wrath of God will be poured out on the world before the inauguration of the Millennial Kingdom. However, the church will be secretly "raptured" from the earth beforehand to be with Jesus until He returns to establish His kingdom and judge all people.

- **Post-millennialists** see the millennium as an era or an age, not necessarily as a literal one thousand years. During this era, Jesus will rule and reign over the earth through advancing the church by proclaiming the gospel. This will bring about an ever-increasing kingdom reality which will set the stage for the return of Christ, also called a "realized eschatology."

- **A-millennialism** (A = no) is a school of thought that believes Jesus is presently ruling and reigning through the church. A-millennialists see the thousand years as a metaphor for the current church age and await the culmination of all things when Jesus returns.

- The **pan-millennial** view believes everything will "pan out in the end." Nobody knows when Jesus is coming back![9]

Regardless of one's personal eschatological view, the believer's primary focus should center on the work and mission of Jesus Christ.

CHAPTER ONE

A Vision of Christ

Revelation: Is it the unveiling of Jesus Christ, or an unveiling from Jesus Christ?

The revelation from Jesus Christ, which God gave him to show his servants what must soon take place.
— Revelation 1:1 (NIV)

Revelation 1:1 begins with a statement: John was communicating a message from Jesus to seven churches that were stuck and needed encouragement to continue the work set out for them. The inspiration that moves them to remain faithful is none other than the presence of Jesus Christ Himself in the church. This is thus both a revelation *of* Jesus Christ and a revelation *from* Jesus Christ.

This unveiling of Christ which the Father "gave him to show to his servants" (anyone who believes) is "what must soon take place." The end of this first verse in

Revelation has sparked denominational disputes over interpretation: When is He coming back? Since Jesus ascended, there have been no fewer than three hundred failed attempts to predict the second coming of Christ, particularly around millennial turns.

False predictions have abounded for centuries because God's people aren't supposed to predict. Jesus was clear His return would come "like a thief in the night" (1 Thessalonians 5:2). Building a church around "what must soon take place," (end-times scenarios) rather than on the person of Jesus will open up endless interpretive possibilities, and divert people's attention. Jesus must be the epicenter of interpretation, and will certainly be for the purposes of this book.

The Blessings of the Revelation (Right Off the Bat)

The first blessing appears at the beginning of John's letter: "Blessed is the one who reads aloud the words of this prophecy, and blessed are those who hear it and take to heart what is written in it" (Revelation 1:3 NIV).

This means at this very moment, God will pour out blessing after blessing after blessing to anyone who reads and hears Revelation and takes to heart what is written in it. They will be blessed when they actually live out the apocalyptic vision God is breathing through this book.

This revelation matters tremendously to God, but for too long it has been relegated to something terrifying and foreboding—and something misinterpreted. John's letter was supposed to inspire God's people. It was supposed to encourage the church, and unleash the Holy Spirit in its midst because God is the one who provides blessings in a person's life. This revelation was intended to anchor people to Jesus since the whole book is about Him, from beginning to end.

John's salutation in Revelation 1:4 clearly communicated who his audience is:

> *To the seven churches in the province of Asia: Grace and peace to you from him who is, and who was, and who is to come, and from the seven spirits[a] before his throne, and from Jesus Christ, who is the faithful witness, the firstborn from the dead, and the ruler of the kings of the earth. To him who loves us and has freed us from our sins by his blood.* — **Revelation 1:4–5 (NIV)**

John was writing to the seven churches in the province of Asia or the western part of modern-day Turkey. John also made it clear the revelation was not from him, but from Jesus, "who is, and who was, and who is to come."

John was merely the transmitter of the revelation, the one who was testifying to the vision of Christ. The Greek word used for "witness" actually means "martyr."[10] Jesus was the faithful martyr even unto death.

He was faithful to carry out what His Father willed. He didn't cut it short. Jesus is also the "firstborn of the dead," the first of many to be resurrected from death to life (Revelation 1:5 NIV). He did not die again but remains alive and in you who believe by the power of the

Holy Spirit. Because He has conquered death, He is the ruler of the kings on earth.

Because of His faithful and unending love for you, He has also freed you from your sins, "by his blood" (Revelation 1:5 NIV). You no longer remain in your sins. Your hurts, hang-ups, or bad habits are not your identity. When you believed Jesus is the Savior, your identity became one who is loved by God, no matter where you've been and no matter what you've done. How is that possible? Only by the blood of Christ. His sacrifice has freed you from your sin. You have been made part of His kingdom, the church.

When Jesus Comes to Church

Imagine being captive in a cool, dark cave. Smell the musty earth and feel the crumbling dirt and rocks—nowhere to sit but the hard ground, and no one to talk to but the Lord. Now, picture John on his knees, turning his prison into a holy place.

In Revelation 1:9, John said, "I, John, your brother and companion in the suffering and kingdom and patient endurance that are ours in Jesus, was on the island of Patmos because of the word of God and the testimony of Jesus" (NIV). From the first drops of ink on the papyrus, John identified himself with the people who were feeling pressure from the Roman emperor, Domitian. They were suffering for their faith, and John wanted them to know he was too.

The word "suffering" in Revelation 1:9 is the Greek word *thlipsis*, also translated "tribulation."[11] It means,

"A pressing together, literally or figuratively; anguish, burdened, persecution or trouble."

Has anyone ever tried to comfort you when you were in a difficult spot, even though they had never experienced a similar trial in their life? Perhaps they offered what they thought would be comforting words like, "Oh, it's going to get better, honey," but their words carried no meaning—because in truth, they couldn't relate.

John was trying to offer words of comfort to his audience, but he first made it clear he related with their pain and suffering and could thus empathize with them. He did so by referring to those in the churches as a family. He referred to himself as "your brother and your companion." He was suffering with them, and they with him.

Domitian's rule was ruthless; the Romans crushed in doors, took entire families captive, and killed many.[12] Few in twenty-first century America can relate to this kind of intense persecution; however, imagine those currently living in the Middle East where terrorist groups are known to attack people's homes and families daily. If you were to write a letter to those families, what would you say? How would you write a letter to a Christian family in Iraq whose father has just been beheaded by a militant or whose daughter has been kidnapped, brutalized, and raped?

This was similar to the audience to whom John was writing. Terror, fear, and death were a part of everyday life—all for believing in Jesus.

Before He had been crucified, died, and was buried,
Jesus said:

> *I have told you these things, so that in me you may*
> *have peace. In this world you will have trouble. But*
> *take heart! I have overcome the world.* — **John 16:33**
> **(NIV)**

Trouble is part of the journey. Jesus knew this, but He
assured His followers that when they were walking
through the darkest trials of their life—and they would
come—He was already victorious. He had already
"overcome the world." To preach a gospel that doesn't
speak of Christ's suffering is to preach a different
gospel. Jesus told believers ahead of time they would
have trouble and would face terrible persecution and
possibly even death. Yet He called those who trust in
Him to pick up their crosses and follow Him.

Jesus also knew His followers would survive the
intense tribulation He knew what was ahead on their
own. He knew the persecution would be too much for
any human being to bear. But he comforted His disciples
before leaving this earth saying, "Surely I am with you
always, to the very end of the age" and promised a
comforter who would act as an advocate "to help you
and be with you forever" (John 14:16). This coming
Holy Spirit would whisper to those who were in the
depths of despair, "You're right. You can't bear this. But
God can through you."

John continued his letter to describe when He
received the revelation:

On the Lord's Day I was in the Spirit, and I heard behind me a loud voice like a trumpet. —**Revelation 1:10 (NIV)**

It was "on the Lord's day" that this message from Jesus came. John alluded to the book of Exodus and that unexplainable day in Israel's history when He gave His perfect instruction through Moses. On that day at Mount Sinai, the mountain was engulfed in smoke as the Lord descended upon it in the fire. The mountain quaked violently, and "the sound of the trumpet grew louder and louder" (Ephesians 19:19).

The original hearers of John's letter would likely have recalled Hebrew Scriptures that compared God's booming voice on Mount Sinai to the reverberating sound of a trumpet. Think of ancient biblical times when kings entered a town or processions when the emperor showed up. What heralded those leaders? Trumpets. Kings: Jesus. John's introduction prepared his audience for something profound: he had heard Jesus speak.

By the early second century, the Christian church was calling Sunday the Lord's Day because that was the day Jesus was resurrected. This information is also included in the *Didache,* a book about the teachings of the early church. But the early church still attended synagogue on the Saturday, or "Sabbath" (in Hebrew, *Shabbat*). The early church first gathered together on Sabbath to focus on worshipping Christ. But by the second century, the Christian church had become more established. Man's traditions crept in, and worship switched from Saturday to Sunday.[13]

Of more importance than what day it was, were John's words—that he was *"in the Spirit"* (Revelation 1:10 NIV). John was in such a place with the Lord, so removed from the distractions of people and responsibilities that he was almost in a different realm. Though John was in exile—until Emperor Domitian died and he was released to spend the rest of his days in Ephesus[14]—he remained in the spirit.

In the Spirit in the Midst of Exile

Do you feel like you're isolated in a sea of people who are against you? Maybe you feel like you never have enough energy beyond just getting through the day and are not fully engaged in life. Or you've been turned down by company after company after company. You might be struggling with depression, which has created a "Patmos" of its own in your life, your own "exile."

Guess what? In the middle of that island, God wants to bring you His Spirit. The Holy Spirit is alive and well, and if God's people would allow the Spirit to move, they would be empowered by God day after day. The presence of God dwells within believers and is present even in their most despairing moments. That is the kingdom of God.

Next, John heard a voice commanding him to document what he saw:

Write on a scroll what you see and send it to the seven churches: to Ephesus, Smyrna, Pergamum, Thyatira, Sardis, Philadelphia and Laodicea. I turned

*around to see seven golden lampstands, and among
the lampstands was someone like a son of man,
dressed in a robe reaching down to his feet and with a
golden sash around his chest.* — **Revelation 1:11–13
(NIV)**

In the original Greek, the wording is "what you are
seeing [you] write!" The root word *see* is the word *blepō*,
which means, as one would expect, "to have the faculty
of sight."[15] In Revelation 1:11, it is in the present active
indicative tense, *blepeis*. This indicates John was
charged with documenting the events as he saw them,
scene by scene, while he was in the Spirit.

John continued, describing the details of this person,
who was "like a son of man":

*The hairs of his head were white, like white wool, like
snow. His eyes were like a flame of fire, his feet were
like burnished bronze, refined in a furnace, and his
voice was like the roar of many waters.* — **Revelation
1:14–15 (ESV)**

The recipients of John's letter would have listened to
his words and immediately connected what John was
describing in his vision to an Old Testament prophet,
Daniel. Daniel described a similar vision while his
people, the Israelites, were in Babylonian captivity:

*As I looked, thrones were set in place, and the
Ancient of Days took his seat. His clothing was as
white as snow; the hair of his head was white like
wool. His throne was flaming with fire, and its
wheels were all ablaze. A river of fire was flowing,*

coming out from before him. Thousands upon thousands attended him; ten thousand times ten thousand stood before him. The court was seated, and the books were opened.

Then I continued to watch because of the boastful words the horn was speaking. I kept looking until the beast was slain and its body destroyed and thrown into the blazing fire. (The other beasts had been stripped of their authority, but were allowed to live for a period of time.)

In my vision at night I looked, and there before me was one like a son of man, coming with the clouds of heaven. He approached the Ancient of Days and was led into his presence. **— Daniel 7:9-13 (NIV)**

A few chapters later, Daniel continued his description:

His body was like topaz, his face like lightning, his eyes like flaming torches, his arms and legs like the gleam of burnished bronze, and his voice like the sound of a multitude. I, Daniel, was the only one who saw this vision. **— Daniel 10:6–7 (NIV)**

This was Daniel's vision, but somewhere around 435 years later,[16] John saw the same vision: "The hairs of his head were white, like white wool, like snow" (Revelation 1:14 ESV).

Daniel and John were describing the face of God. Throughout the Old Testament, it is clear God's people could not see God. In Deuteronomy 4:12, Moses wrote that the Lord spoke from the midst of the fire with audible words, but "you saw no form—only a voice"

(NASB) and in Exodus 33:20 God said, "You cannot see My face, for no man can see Me and live!" (NASB). However, Daniel and John described God's face. How is this possible?

Hebrews 1:3 and Colossians 1:15 declare Jesus is the exact representation of the invisible God. When someone sees Jesus, they've seen the Father. The first two verses of the book of Hebrews discuss how God has finally revealed Himself through His son, Jesus Christ. Even Jesus declared, "Whoever has seen me, has seen the Father" (John 14:9 ESV).

John's letter opened with profound information for the seven churches. He had seen God, in the person of Jesus Christ. Surely this grabbed his readers' and listeners' attention, which likely was John's intent. For after his introduction, John followed with harsh words.

Chapter One Questions

Question: Can you identify a time when you did not feel comforted by someone because they had not experienced your pain personally?

_____

_____

_____

_____

_____

_____

_____

_____

_____

_____

Question: What does Jesus look like in your mind's eye? Where do you think this image comes from?

_____

_____

_____

_____

_____

_____

_____

_____

_____

_____

Action: Live as though you have been blessed through the unveiling of Christ because you have been! Use the book of Revelation to be inspired, encouraged, and uplifted. It is time to use this gift as God intended.

Chapter One Notes

CHAPTER TWO

The Incarnational Church

The church is more than brick and mortar, and far more than a structure. But sometimes people (and leaders) within the church forget this truth. The sun comes up on Sunday morning and husbands and wives, moms and dads, parents and children ask, "Hey, are we going to church?" Immediately an image or a picture of a building pops into people's minds—not a global community of people.

In the Greek, the word for "church" is *ekklēsia*, which means "a gathering of people called out into community who are traveling and doing life together."[17] The church is a called-out people, and yet is empowered to be incarnational—to immerse itself in the local culture and show Jesus to that culture. In other words, believers are "called out" as a group of people who belong to God, who have been empowered by the presence of the Holy Spirit in their midst, and to be the "incarnational" representation of Christ.[18]

When Jesus came to earth the first time as a baby, born in Bethlehem, the term used is "the incarnation." This describes when God became human and dwelt among humanity. When people receive Jesus Christ as Lord and Savior, they become "incarnational." This means they become portals for the divine life of Christ to move in and through them, to affect other people.

The church is called and empowered to be incarnational within its current culture, neighborhood, community, city, or town. The context of the believer's mission is to love as Christ loves. Jesus' entire ministry was motivated by compassion and love for people. His work on earth wasn't duty, and it wasn't doctrine; it was all based on love.

The 5P Template

The way Jesus addressed the seven churches was similar to how Persian and Roman kingdoms in ancient biblical times issued decrees. Back then, a king's decree was typically mixed with a prophetic oracle. It follows this format:

- Place
- Picture
- Praise
- Problem
- Prescription

In the same way, John's letter addressed each church in the letter using this pattern. John first identified a church (place), described an image (picture), commended the church for what it was doing right (praise), presented what the church was doing wrong (problem) and then told the church how to solve the issue at hand (prescription).

As John's letter of Revelation was being read to each church, its people heard everything Jesus said regarding the other churches—good and bad. Likely there were awkward moments, especially when a church was reprimanded. I imagine them turning to one another, saying, "I'm glad that one wasn't us. At least we didn't do *that*."

Remember, those seven churches weren't the only churches that existed at the time. There were probably well over one hundred small fellowships by this point. Eventually, the seven churches mentioned in Revelation would have multiplied and continued to spread. As these churches expanded, the global church swelled as well.

Hallmarks of the Church of Ephesus

Revelation 2 begins with a message to a church familiar to students of the Bible: the church of Ephesus. At the time, Ephesus was the center of travel and commerce—an incredible crossroads of a city. The apostle Paul had started a church in Ephesus years before John wrote Revelation.

While in Corinth, Paul had become friends with a believing couple named Aquila and Priscilla. When Paul left Corinth to travel to Ephesus, a city on the western coast of what is modern-day Turkey, he took Aquila and Priscilla with him (Act 18:18 NIV).

A Jew named Apollos came to Ephesus, and though he knew the Hebrew Scriptures and "had been instructed in the way of the Lord" (Acts 18:25 NIV), he did not know about the baptism of the Holy Spirit. Aquila and Priscilla brought him into their home—which was perhaps a place of fellowship and worship for followers of Jesus—and "explained to him the way of God more adequately (Acts 18:26 NIV).

Later on, Paul returned to Ephesus and spent more time with that church than any other churches, developing and discipling the people for three years. He appointed Timothy as the lead pastor in the church of Ephesus urging Timothy to "commend certain persons not to teach false doctrines any longer" (1 Timothy 1:3–4 NIV). Many believe that when John went to Ephesus, he was accompanied by Mary, Jesus' mother.[19] Recall that as He was hanging on the cross, Jesus chose John out of all the disciples, commissioning him to look after His mother when He was gone (John 19:26–27).

Imagine being in a church with that type of leadership: Paul, Aquila, Priscilla, Apollos, Timothy, John, and Mary, the mother of God? It was to this group of leaders, and the entire congregation at Ephesus that Paul wrote in his letter:

For this reason, ever since I heard about your faith in the Lord Jesus and your love for all God's people, I have not stopped giving thanks for you, remembering you in my prayers. —**Ephesians 1:15–16 (NIV)**

Paul noted the entire church in Ephesus exhibited an incredible love for all of God's people. They were strong, and steadfast in faith. And they knew God's Word.

Not surprisingly, there were things working against the city of Ephesus spiritually because of its dominant position in the world at that time. Ephesus was a powerful city within the Roman Empire in what was called Asia Minor, the primary port where ships docked for trade and commerce. It was also the bridge city between the East and the West. At one point, the Roman Empire extended from Britain all the way to India. So powerful was Ephesus the city was dubbed, "the Light of Asia."[20]

One of the largest theaters ever built in the Roman Empire existed in Ephesus, able to seat up to twenty-five thousand people. Known as "The Great Theater of Ephesus,"[21] it could host Olympic-style games. The population of Ephesus was more than a quarter of a million people at the time—a sizeable city—but at the height of the games, more than two million people would flood its streets and pile into the theater to watch the games.

Despite its size and power, even the poets of the time knew how spiritually dark Ephesus was. Within the prominent temple of Artemis, also called the temple of Diana, cult prostitution was prolific.

Murder was common and frequent. Because of this, Ephesus became known (in the way Las Vegas is notorious today) for its immoral activity.[22]

Still, it was a strategic city and establishing a church in Ephesus was profoundly wise. The light of Christ would emanate through this church which existed at the crossroads between the East and West. It is not surprising, then, that the Ephesian church (along with the others mentioned in the letter) experienced intense persecution and crushing under Roman rule. This was why John communicated his revelation to the church in Ephesus.

One of the main reasons the Ephesians suffered persecution at this particular time was because of Domitian. Domitian was known for his cruelty—he slaughtered anyone who was a threat to his rule. Domitian's barbarism and brutality escalated to an entirely new level surpassing all other leaders. He demanded to be called Dominus Et Deus, which means, "master and God."[23] Under Domitian's rule, the cult of emperor worship escalated to new heights—for Domitian sought to be worshipped as a living god.

The Agora in Ephesus was the designated area for commerce. It was a massive area, the most important trade center of the city. Merchants sold food, fabric, clothing, and other goods here—and thus, the Agora was paramount for life in Ephesus.

Domitian knew this and used it to his advantage. Recall Domitian demanded his people worship him as lord and god. All patrons were required to light incense in honor of the divinity of Domitian to be allowed entrance to the Agora.[24] To the Jew and the Christian, this was utterly unacceptable. However, refusal meant a person or family went without necessary items for survival—even food. If parents were unwilling to worship Domitian, their kids would go hungry or cold. Sneaking into the market was near impossible, for each person who made their incense and worship offerings to Domitian was marked. Jews and Christians wouldn't have taken this mark to be able to buy, sell, and trade; this meant they would be selling out their faith and beliefs.

However, this was everyday life for people in Ephesus. Anyone who refused to receive the mark of Domitian was rounded up and executed; Domitian feared followers of Jesus would usurp his throne.

The Caesar Lineage

At this point, it's helpful to understand Caesar's lineage. Julius Caesar ruled Rome until about 44 BC,[25] followed by Augustus who ruled from 27 BC to about AD 14. Caesar Augustus would have been the man on the throne during the birth of Christ.[26] Augustus died right around the turn of the century.

Tiberius took over the throne from AD 14–37. The people believed Augustus was a god, and naturally, Tiberius took on the title of "son of god."[27] It was about this time things grew interesting as prophecies and pagan practices began to bubble up foretelling, "Someone is about to come into the world and create a huge shift that is going to bring about a reign of peace and righteousness on the earth." This was what the Hebrew Scriptures said about the coming Jewish Messiah. People began to ask, "Are you the one who is to come?"

John the Baptist heard about what Jesus was doing while sitting in prison. This was why he sent a letter to Jesus echoing the same question: "Are you the one who is to come, or should we expect someone else?" (Matthew 11:3 NIV).

Caligula rose to power next, another terrible and wicked leader. Caligula ruled from AD 37–41. Claudius followed from AD 41–54.[28]

Following Caligula, one of Rome's most infamous leaders ascended to power: Nero. Nero, known for his corruption and for his appalling persecution of Christians, reigned from AD 54–68.[29] After Nero died, there were three emperors who took control of Rome in very short succession; two were murdered, and one committed suicide. Galba ruled for about seven months before he was executed, while Otho committed suicide after three months. Vitellius lived about eight months before he was executed. Like Tiberius, these Caesars bought into the idea that they were gods. Caesar worship continued to intensify.[30]

Vespasian ruled from AD 68–79, and was known for overseeing decent things for Rome,[31] and persecution decreased for a season. However, Vespasian's son, Titus, succeeded him, best known for destroying Jerusalem in AD 70.[32]

Titus had a brother whose name was Domitian. When Titus died in AD 81, Domitian took the throne. More than any of the other Caesars, Domitian wanted to be known as master and god. He created the Domitian games, which rivaled the Olympics. He built massive theaters to hold the games as well as other gladiatorial events.

At the games, Domitian sat high up on a pedestal. Everyone, including spectators, donned white robes; Domitian's priests boasted golden crowns embellished with his name across their foreheads. The priests honored Domitian as master, god, and the lord of light. They sang songs to him during the events; this was also how spectators gained entrance to the games.

To initiate the start of the games, leaders from different regions around the world would come and present themselves before Domitian. Domitian would declare to each leader, "Here is what I have *for* you, and here's what I have *against* you." Leader after leader would bow before Domitian to receive his decree.[33]

Tuck these images away for now. They will resurface numerous times throughout the book of Revelation.

Do You Know Who I Am?

With that background, it's time to study Ephesus in its proper context. John began with a picture of Jesus to open his letter:

> *To the angel of the church in Ephesus write: These are the words of him who holds the seven stars in his right hand and walks among the seven golden lampstands. — Revelation 2:1 (NIV)*

The golden lampstands refer to the church. Back in Revelation 1:12, Jesus had declared the seven golden lampstands "are the seven churches" (NIV). Thus, John's image of Jesus walking "among the seven golden lampstands" communicated a beautiful picture of Jesus' presence in the church.

The "angel of the church in Ephesus" was likely a reference to the lead pastor of the church. The seven stars represented the leaders from those seven churches. Through his apostle, Jesus was saying, "I am in control, but I am not distant. I am as close as you need me to be."

Jesus next said:

> *I know your works, your toil, your patient endurance and how you cannot bear with those who are evil but have tested those who call themselves apostles and are not, and you found them to be false. —* **Revelation 2:2 (ESV)**

The word "know" in the phrase, "I know your works" refers to a comprehensive knowing. When I first became a Christian, one of the things that concerned me the most was that Jesus saw my every move, whether I was doing good things or bad things. That was a scary proposition for me to weigh.

Consider the story of a young man who was experiencing his first week away from college. He had an incredible week. He met his new roommate; they went to all of the orientations together. At the end of the week, they looked forward to attending a final reception before classes started. The young man was milling around when a woman came up to him initiating a conversation.

The woman asked the young man, "So, are you enjoying your experience at school?" The young man answered, "Oh, it's awesome!" She responded, "Is there anything you don't like?" He said, "Well, everything is pretty good. The only thing I don't like is the president of the school." Taken aback a little, she asked, "What don't you like about the president?"

He answered, "He just seems so aloof and disconnected, and he doesn't seem to really know what he's doing. I am not even sure if he can really run the place."

The lady said, "Young man, do you have any idea who I am? I am the president's wife, and I can't believe you just said that!"

The young man looked at her and asked, "Well, do you have any idea who I am?"

She shook her head.

Relieved, he responded, "Good!" and ran away.

As that young man could attest, sometimes it's best when others don't know everything about a person—but Jesus does.

The Problem

John quickly moved on to the problem: the Ephesian church had left something it was well known for: "But I have this against you, that you have abandoned the love you had at first," Jesus said (Revelation 2:4 NIV).

This was a love that overflowed from the church as a result of their salvation. Recall the kind of love that characterized the Ephesians—a love that was reflected in the joy resulting from a deep understanding of the significance of what it meant to be brought from death to life.

Now, only a few decades later, Jesus declared the Ephesians had lost this pure, unadulterated love. They had become heresy hunters. The Ephesians' fatal flaw was one all believers need to be careful of.

Perhaps you have encountered a person who focused more on whose sin was worse or whose doctrines were wrong than on Jesus. Such a person, according to Jesus in Revelation 2, has a fatal flaw. The person may know the Scriptures; they may have studied the Scriptures; they may have been able to bullhorn truth all over the world, but they still have a fatal flaw because knowing the Bible is not enough. Being the church means reflecting Christ's love, compassion, and mercy to a lost world.

This is the key question all believers should ask themselves: *Do I love like Christ?*

Do I not only know what's true but do I also extend grace to people who don't agree with my truth? Can I determine right teaching from incorrect teaching, yet still possess and pour out love and grace?

It is easy to look at the church and conclude of its people, "They are so judgmental. I love Jesus; I just don't like the church. I'd rather hike up a mountain today and worship there, or go worship on the golf course." But the reality is Christians cannot grow in love and grace apart from the community of faith. That's how God designed it. Growth does not happen in isolation.

John next relayed what Jesus said was the prescription for the problem: to remember, repent, and return. "Remember therefore from where you have fallen; repent, and do the works you did at first. If not, I will come to you and remove your lampstand from its place, unless you repent" (Revelation 2:5 ESV). I can still remember my first days of being a Christian. It was thrilling to go the Christian bookstore, buy Christian records, listen to sermons, and talk about God with other followers of Jesus. Everything was new. Everything was fresh. I talked to everybody I encountered about Jesus. I couldn't get enough!

I looked for ways to bless people, to perform acts of service for others, just so I could tell them that Jesus loved them. Now, however, my attitude has shifted. Often, when I am weary from ministry, I don't patiently endure like the Ephesians. It is in those moments I am reminded of the need to rekindle my first love. If this sounds like you, too, make the decision to repent.

Jesus left the Ephesian church with a promise if it repented: "He who has an ear, let him hear what the Spirit says to the churches. To the one who conquers I will grant to eat of the tree of life, which is in the paradise of God" (Revelation 2:7 ESV). For followers of Christ, this promise remains true as well.

The phrase "he who has an ear, let him hear" appears fourteen times in the Bible. When God repeats a word or a phrase, He intends for readers to pay attention. Believers in Christ would do well to apply this concept in Revelation 2:7 to their own lives: *If you have ears, listen up.*

How are you doing? Are you listening? Have you been so focused on being doctrinally pure that it has affected your ability to extend love and grace? If so, you have a fatal flaw, which can separate you from Christ. Don't turn a deaf ear to this sobering truth.

WORKBOOK

Chapter Two Questions

Question: What does the word church mean for you? Is it more than a place or a building for you? What does "church" represent?

_____

_____

_____

_____

_____

_____

_____

_____

_____

_____

_____

Question: How is the present-day church similar to the church of Ephesus?

_____

_____

_____

_____

_____

_____

_____

_____

_____

_____

Question: As a Christian, has your focus been predominantly on grace, or on sin?

_____

_____

_____

_____

_____

_____

_____

_____

_____

_____

_____

Action: The church was never meant to be just a building. It is time to encourage the church to become what it was meant to be—the hands and feet of Jesus— and focus on grace instead of sin.

Chapter Two Notes

CHAPTER THREE

Smyrna—Faithful Under Pressure

God intercepts people right where they are. John's letter to the churches was no exception. While the message to the church at Ephesus encouraged believers to grow and abound in love and grace, the letter to the church at Smyrna encouraged believers to be strong and faithful while undergoing weighty persecution.

About Smyrna

Smyrna has an interesting history dating to about 1000 BC. Around 600 BC, the Lydians destroyed the great city, and it was only under Greece that it came back to life. Many believed Smyrna was the home of Homer, the writer and philosopher of *The Iliad.* Today the city is called Izmir, a city in Turkey.[34]

Like Ephesus, Smyrna was also a powerful city, and because of this, not surprisingly, the two cities experienced some rivalry. Both were port cities (centers of merchandise and trade) on the East–West divide. What Smyrna boasted that Ephesus did not was a double port. The city enjoyed a secure harbor, and its port was even grander than the port of Ephesus. Upon pulling into the port, one was welcomed with vibrant green hills dotted with temples erected to various gods—like a metaphorical crown.[35]

Smyrna's people were also involved in emperor worship more than the Ephesians were. Any resident of Smyrna who did not bow the knee to the emperor and call him "lord" was summarily executed.[36]

Of the seven churches mentioned in Revelation, only two still exist: Smyrna and Philadelphia. Interestingly, these churches were the only two of the seven Jesus said nothing negative about.[37]

Thlipsis

John continued, addressing the church at Smyrna: "I know your afflictions and your poverty—yet you are rich! I know about the slander of those who say they are Jews and are not, but are a synagogue of Satan" (Revelation 2:9 NIV).

Jesus was not unaware of what the people of the church at Smyrna had experienced. He used the word afflictions, which is often translated as tribulation, which is the Greek word *thlipsis* which means, "pressure."[38]

When examined further, *thlipsis* presents an image of two or more things being pressed together. Take for example the olive press. Before producing olive oil, the olive is placed under a weight, which crushes the olive's skin. Though the skin remains, the oil begins to flow just like juice flows from the grape. Interestingly, Gethsemane—the garden where Jesus spent the last hours of His life praying to His father before being crucified—means *the olive press.* What Jesus experienced in the garden was crushing. Jesus knows when His people feel persecuted, it is like being crushed like the olive.

Have you ever felt like the pressures of life weighed so heavily on you, crushing you to the point where it was almost hard to breathe? Perhaps you wondered, "Does God even know? Does *anybody* know?" Often people think if they are experiencing *thlipsis*—they are going through a trying time—they must have done something wrong when in reality, life is simply hard.

Consider Job, an Old Testament prophet whose life illustrated that sometimes bad things happen even when a person is doing everything right. Suffering exists because sin exists.

Job had done everything right. He was holy. He was righteous. He pleased God; there was nothing wrong in his life—but then the bottom fell out, and he lost everything. Job was devastated, and God was silent. Then, as he was licking his wounds and pulling himself out of the pit, the bottom fell out again.

And God was *still* silent.

On top of his deep grief and pain, his close friends responded by saying, "Hey, God is just working out His plan in your life."

Sometimes life involves *thlipsis* or tribulation. And though it might not be what God desires, it may be what He allows.

Suffering is an unpleasant but necessary part of life, while at the same time, it is what produces the quickest growth. The apostle Paul wrote of suffering:

> *We rejoice in our sufferings, knowing that suffering produces endurance, and endurance produces character, and character produces hope, and hope does not put us to shame, because God's love has been poured into our hearts through the Holy Spirit who has been given to us.* — **Romans 5:3–5 (NIV)**

Ultimately, suffering produces character which in turn produces hope. And for this reason, suffering is not always something negative.

For example, when tragedy strikes a community such as a natural disaster or a death, people often begin to unite with each other. Relationships are deepened, and the result is a closer community.

In the West, people don't experience *thlipsis* the same way people in the church at Smyrna did. They certainly don't experience *thlipsis* the same way Christians in other countries do. Christians today are the most persecuted religious group in the world, but most Americans are unaware. An average of at least 180 Christians around the world are killed each month for their faith.[39]

Persecution in the West, though it exists, is an entirely different level of persecution and nowhere near what

Christian brothers and sisters all over the globe experience.

One early church historian, Tertullian, wrote: "If the Tiber rises too high for the walls, or the Nile too low for the fields ... instantly the howl is, 'The Christians to the lion!'"[40] This was the mindset back then, and the reality of life for many within the early church. Christians were the most marginalized group. To profess faith openly and in public meant certain death in many situations.

When the earliest Christians showed up at church, they looked around the room to see who was missing from last week. That person they had prayed with the week before might have been murdered. Maybe the person they gave clothing to was missing in the lineup. Problems for Christians in churches today are mostly first-world problems.

This church at Smyrna, however, was experiencing *thlipsis*.

Poverty and No Way Out

Not only did the Christians in Smyrna experience intense pressure from the outside, but they were terribly impoverished and destitute. They were marginalized; business owners did not hire Christians. The Jews didn't like the Christians because they were Gentiles who claimed to follow a Jewish Messiah. On top of that, Rome despised those who followed Jesus.

In his commentary on Revelation, William Barclay highlighted six things Christians were constantly accused of that resulted in execution.[41] Note that imprisonment was typically the gateway to execution.

1. Cannibalism

Christians were accused of cannibalism because of the sacrament of communion—eating the body and drinking the blood of Jesus Christ.

2. Agape Feasts

Agape is a Greek word meaning, "Love without condition." To the outsider, Christians conducted services known as love feasts or "agape feasts." Non-believers tried to twist the intent of these gatherings, accusing participants of drunken sexual orgies (as if that wasn't happening in every one of their temples). This incensed people who saw these feasts as a reason to arrest Christians.

3. Divided Families

If someone became a Christian, their family extricated themselves from their son, daughter, or parent. Belief in Jesus Christ divided families.

4. Atheism

Because Christians didn't worship a man-made idol, plaque, or image, non-Christians said, "They are atheists; they don't even believe in the gods."

5. Political Dissension

Because early Christians didn't worship Caesar as Lord, they didn't fall in line with Rome.

6. Creating Fear

Christians were accused of stirring up fear in others, declaring the world would one day end up in fire and flames.

The Prescription

Through John's revelation, Jesus called Christians to eliminate *thlipsis* and poverty as best they could and to be an extension of God's love in the world. Remember, Jesus had no criticism for the church at Smyrna. He did, however, provide them two bits of advice to help alleviate their situation:

First, Jesus said, "Do not be afraid of what you are about to suffer" (Revelation 2:10 NIV). This is a hard phrase to embrace. In the West, people expect the words, "Don't be afraid," to be followed with comforting words like, "I am going to get you out of this." People try to avoid suffering at all costs—they peruse Christian self-help bookshelves in bookstores seeking any possible way to avoid suffering. But this was not what Jesus taught, and certainly not what was revealed in the book of Revelation. Christ said not to be afraid of what Christians were about to suffer. These were hard words for the church to receive, but they were the truth. Jesus was not going to come and rescue them—at least not in the way they hoped.

Next, Jesus told the believers in Smyrna, "Be thou faithful unto death, and I will give thee a crown of life" (Revelation 2:10 KJV). Recall that Smyrna was known as "the Crown of Asia."[42] The Bible speaks of several different crowns such as the "crown of glory" and the "crown of righteousness." John alludes to those crowns by speaking of a literal crown to make a clear point: those believers who would be faithful unto death would receive from God the ultimate crown—the crown of life.

The Benefits of Suffering

Suffering is a hard concept to process. It's a part of life, but not one people readily accept. Most hope life will be comfortable. When plans unravel, life gets tangled, and suffering is the new normal, most people point to God and say, "This wasn't *my* plan." However, there are benefits to suffering.

Suffering leads to honesty. When in the midst of suffering, people are sometimes forced to be honest with themselves and others—often for the first time in their lives. Suffering forces people to slow down, or even to function at a different level.

Suffering alters plans. Suffering is a sort of "holy distortion"—a moment or season that can't be changed and will lead to a life forever changed. Instantly a loved one is gone, passing away from a terrible illness. A prodigal child cuts off ties with a parent. A beloved relationship is severed. These "holy distortions" happen, but they are never planned.

Suffering moves people toward solidarity with one another. Suffering unifies people in a way nothing else can, creating solidarity. Solidarity is why the church in Smyrna still has a lampstand in modern-day Izmir. Solidarity is why Polycarp said, "For eighty-six years have I served him [Christ]. How can I blaspheme my King and Savior?"[43]

Suffering is a part of the journey. Jesus doesn't remove suffering, for without suffering, growth remains dormant. Suffering is a necessary part of life, but it is the part people would rather do without; it's the book never bought, the radio station turned off.

If you are feeling the *thlipsis*—the pressure, the crush—Jesus is whispering in your ear right now, "I know how you feel."

What Myrrh Has to Do with It

Smyrna means "myrrh."[44] Myrrh was one of the three gifts the Magi brought to Jesus:

> *On coming to the house, they saw the child with his mother Mary, and they bowed down and worshiped him. Then they opened their treasures and presented him with gifts of gold, frankincense and myrrh... —* **Matthew 2:11 (NIV)**

Frankincense in the Scriptures pointed to the priestly role Jesus would embody in his life. Gold represented His royalty, and myrrh alluded to the prophetic death Messiah would have to endure so that even when God's people were in exile, they could be free in the spirit. Myrrh is basically hardened tree sap or bark from bushy trees common to Israel.[45]

Regardless of what a person is currently experiencing, no matter how broken or distressed they are, Jesus understands and says, "I was broken too." Myrrh, an anointing oil, emitted a strong, sweet fragrance[46] when ground with pressure against another hard surface. The aroma that flowed from it was phenomenal.

Jesus was affirming the Christians of Smyrna, "I know you are like myrrh. I know you have been crushed, but your lampstand (church) will remain in place. I have nothing against you because you are allowing the beauty of God to be the fragrance of your story."

Jesus' promise to the church of Smyrna is a promise for the church today; no tear will ever be wasted. Each trial, all suffering, and every pain will find a redemptive purpose in Christ. It is the promise that even though people are blemished, every blemish is for a reason. Jesus loves and cherishes those who believe and follow Him.

WORKBOOK

Chapter Three Questions

Question: What have been your greatest times of *thlipsis*?

_____

_____

_____

_____

_____

_____

_____

_____

_____

_____

Question: What has been a "myrrh" experience in your life—when has beauty or redemption followed a crushing blow?

_____

_____

_____

_____

_____

_____

_____

_____

_____

_____

_____

_____

Question: When has someone rescued you from the "olive press" of life? What do you remember most about their actions and how they made you feel?

_____

_____

_____

_____

_____

_____

_____

_____

_____

_____

_____

_____

Action: Suffering is meant to produce fruit in the Christian life and is never meaningless or useless to God. Claim this truth, and look for the fruit in all circumstances.

Chapter Three Notes

CHAPTER FOUR

Pergamum—Everything Is Okay Here

Pergamum was a city whose people honestly believed they were doing all the right things. Jesus affirmed this church for remaining true to His name and did not renounce faith in Him according to Revelation 2:12–13. However, something had gone awry, reflected in His next words to this church:

> *Nevertheless, I have a few things against you: There are some among you who hold to the teaching of Balaam, who taught Balak to entice the Israelites to sin so that they ate food sacrificed to idols and committed sexual immorality. Likewise, you also have those who hold to the teaching of the Nicolaitans. Repent therefore! Otherwise, I will soon come to you and will fight against them with the sword of my mouth.* **— Revelation 2:14–15 (NIV)**

John MacArthur said, "No one sets out to become an apostate. It's never the result of one abrupt drastic turn away from the Lord. Instead, apostasy is most often the product of a pattern of sinful compromises that harden and gradually steer a professing believer away from the truth."[47] Apostasy never happens immediately. A person doesn't wake up one morning and say, "I don't want to follow Christ anymore." Often, while thinking things are going well, sin lures believers in a direction they never thought they would—which is exactly what happened to the church in Pergamum.

Vegas of the Ancient World

About seventy miles north of Smyrna was the church at Pergamum, near the modern-day city of Bergama, Turkey. Pergamum was the center of all culture.[48] Though not a port city, it was the first city inland from the Aegean Sea. Everything that really happened in Roman culture took place in Pergamum, which can be likened to a modern-day Vegas or Hollywood; many diverse cultures and nationalities contributed to the makeup of a lively society.

Pergamum was known as the greatest city in Asia. It was a fortress perched high on a hilltop that overlooked the surrounding valley. Because the city was a convergence for so many different cultures, peoples, and races, it naturally bred a variety of worship practices; there were numerous temples erected to different gods and a bounty of other atrocities the city's people could worship.

Pergamum boasted a library that held over 200,000 documents in it.[49] The city was filled with beautiful architectural features—baths, temples, sanctuaries, and palaces. In the midst of this giant "melting pot" is where the church at Pergamum started.

The picture John painted in Revelation 2:12–13 cuts to the heart: "These are the words of him who has the sharp, double-edged sword. I know where you live—where Satan has his throne" (NIV). Pergamum offered a smattering of gods to meet anyone's personal worship needs. There was the altar to Zeus and a huge healing center for Asclepius, which is the original fountain of youth.[50] These areas would be filled with beds where a person could lie down and rest, have their dreams interpreted, or try new medicines. Modern-day spas are not far off from what existed back in ancient Pergamum.

There was also emperor worship, with an altar to the ruling emperor of the time. Those who risked rebelling against emperor worship knew their lives were in jeopardy. The other altar was at the temple of Dionysius, the god of wine[51] who was often portrayed with bull horns. Dionysus was long associated with drunkenness, fertility, and madness.

This is the environment in which the church of Pergamum was trying to follow Jesus. But Jesus knew all they were up against. As Luke wrote, "And the very hairs on your head are all numbered. So don't be afraid; you are more valuable to God than the whole flock of sparrows" (Luke 12:7 NLT). Jesus understands where

His people are in their relationship with Him, just as He understood where the church at Pergamum was and what they were going through. As I read this passage in Luke, I was reminded and encouraged that God knows exactly where I am today, even in the most minor of things.

The principle of the Christian life is not one of escape, but of conquest. Though Jesus is well aware of what His children are going through, the response should not be to run away from difficulties but to run to Him. Some might succumb to an attitude that says, "Whoa, my faith is pushing me to do too much!" but Jesus calls believers to move forward and conquer.

Perhaps this is why He, Jesus, began His message to the church of Pergamum saying, "I know where you dwell" (Revelation 2:13 ESV). In other words, "I know you are living right where Satan is worshipped." Regardless, Jesus knew these believers were able to conquer.

Standing Up for Faith

In spite of where the people of Pergamum lived, "where Satan has his throne," (Revelation 2:12), John next praised those believers for standing firm. He continued: "Yet you remain true to my name" (Revelation 2:13 NIV). Through John, Jesus encouraged believers, commending them for not denying their faith in spite of such dark surrounding influences.

But then John jumped to another character named Antipas whom Jesus called, "my faithful witness" and who "was put to death in your city—where Satan lives"

(Revelation 2:13). Now, Antipas was an interesting individual, a man who was dedicated to his faith. In fact, church tradition says John had ordained Antipas as the bishop of Pergamum. Jesus referred to him as being the faithful one who was killed; tradition says Antipas was put to death by being boiled in a copper pot.[52] In the midst of this huge religious, cultural center, Antipas told Christians faith in Jesus had nothing to do with other gods. Because of that, he died a horrible death—supposedly martyred in AD 92.

The rampant apostasy in Pergamum is just as prevalent today. Yet Christians go about their daily lives in Western civilization in comfort, detached from the difficulties of ancient first-century Christians.

Through John, Jesus encouraged the Christians of Pergamum to move forward. Sadly, Christians often reflect a marred image of Christ, mixing in cultural beliefs and tradition with the gospel. Regardless of what some professing Christians say, hold fast to a true faith based on the pure Word of God.

Identifying Problems

After commending the Christians at Pergamum, Jesus then presented the problem:

I have a few things against you: There are some among you who hold the teaching of Balaam, who taught Balak to entice the Israelites to sin so that they ate food sacrificed to idols and committed sexual immorality. — Revelation 2:14 (NIV)

How often, when asked how they are doing, do people respond, "I'm doing great!" when in reality there are deep problems or issues wreaking havoc on their lives. Jesus doesn't avoid the problem; instead, He said something like, "You are doing good, but let me be honest with you; here are some things you need to work on." Then Jesus referenced a man named Balaam.

Balaam was a non-Israelite Old Testament prophet who commenced his prophetic ministry with good intentions. Many people in the ministry today do the same; they think they are doing really good, but slowly allow a temptation, negative influence, or belief contrary to the Word of God to root in and distort their faith.

In Numbers 31, Scripture indicates this is exactly what happened to Balaam: "Behold these, on Balaam's advice, caused the people of Israel to act treacherously against the LORD in the incident of Peor, and so the plague came among the congregation of the LORD" (Numbers 31:16 ESV). Second Peter 2:15 says Balaam "loved the wages of unrighteousness." He was well aware of the dangers of dabbling with the wrong side of God's work, yet continued to seek the reward for the work and not God. Revelation 2:14 says Balaam, "taught Balak to entice the Israelites to sin so that they ate food sacrificed to idols and committed sexual immorality." His behavior provoked God to anger (Numbers 22:22).

In Revelation 2, Jesus didn't say the Christians in Pergamum had completely rebelled, but that they were holding to Balaam's teachings. In other words, they had embraced certain doctrines and beliefs that were slowly drawing them away from God, similar to Balaam.

This slow shifting away from God is happening to American Christians. In the United States, over the course of a few generations, Christians have come to believe what the culture says: Christianity isn't accepted. No one is coming to America saying Christianity is illegal or that it will be eradicated, but still, Christians are embracing ideas and doctrines that weaken their faith.

Are you slowly allowing anything into your life that is taking your focus away from God?

The Prescription

Though some in the church at Pergamum had embraced false teaching, the solution was simple. Jesus said, "Therefore repent" (Revelation 2:16 ESV).

Consider those believers who frequented the city's healing center, or the believers who also worshipped at the emperor's altar. Likely, when they heard John's letter, they thought, "But I still love Jesus!"

Jesus didn't say, "Stop going to that healing center," or "Stop worshipping the emperor." He simply said, "Therefore repent." And in doing so, Jesus revealed three promises that carry over to believers today.

Promise 1: Do it yourself, or I will wage war for you.

Jesus declared "Therefore repent," but immediately followed that statement with a warning: "If not, I will come to you soon and war against them with the sword of my mouth" (Revelation 2:16 ESV). If anyone does not repent upon hearing Jesus' words, He will wage war with those who continue to entice believers away from the faith.

Promise 2: You will receive the hidden manna.

In the next verse, Jesus declared:

> *He who has an ear, let him hear what the Spirit says to the churches. To the one who conquers I will give some of the hidden manna, and I will give him a white stone, with a new name written on the stone that no one knows except the one who receives it. —* **Revelation 2:17 (ESV)**

The book of Exodus tells us that when the Israelites were wandering in the wilderness and had no food, God provided His people with manna (Exodus 16:11–15). Later, in the early sixth century BC, after Solomon's Temple was destroyed, a legend circulated that rabbis took a pot of manna to Mount Sinai and hid it there. They were hiding it for the day the Messiah would come when they would return to that place and share in the blessing of the hidden manna.

The Christians of that time understood the hidden manna had come in the person of Jesus; thus, by following Him, they would receive that hidden blessing the Israelites were waiting for.[53] This second promise to Pergamum and thus to believers today involved blessing for following Jesus.

Promise 3: You will receive a white stone with a new name written on it.

Not only did Jesus promise "hidden manna" to those who overcame the trials of the day, but He promised He would "give him a white stone, with a new name written on the stone that no one knows except the one who receives it" (Revelation 2:17).

Scholars have offered various interpretations for what the "white stone with a new name" meant. The white stone could be referring to a pagan amulet or charm, white marble building materials, or the ancient Roman custom of awarding white stones as prizes at athletic games. Whatever the cultural background, which likely was pagan, Jesus will give those who overcome a new stone engraved with a new name. [54]

When a person puts their faith in Christ, they receive a new name. In the midst of the cultic religious center of Pergamum, Christ promises a new name that no one has seen or understood.

Jesus understands where Christians are coming from but sternly warns against falling away from the faith. It is all too easy to allow subtle influences to shift one's thinking; soon, those ideas seem good when in actuality they have deceptive roots. The prescription is repentance.

Maybe you are so involved in a ministry, or your schedule is so packed you have let the time normally set aside for reading the Bible slip. Or maybe you missed an occasional Sunday from church, which led to missing another and another—and soon it became a habit. Or perhaps you have worked so hard at accepting others in the name of Christian love that you have unknowingly become tolerant of their sin. Jesus addressed this in Revelation 3 in His message to the church at Thyatira. Fervently guard against distractions or attitudes that will divert you from Jesus!

WORKBOOK

Chapter Four Questions

Question: Can you recall a time when you were so busy doing good for God that you stopped following His lead?

_____

_____

_____

_____

_____

_____

_____

_____

_____

_____

_____

Question: When have you moved toward pain instead of from it—persevering to conquer it with God's help?

_____

_____

_____

_____

_____

_____

_____

_____

_____

Question: What new name would you like to see Jesus write on your white stone after you repent? What significance does this name or word hold for you?

_____

_____

_____

_____

_____

_____

_____

_____

_____

_____

Action: Jesus is aware of where you are in your life. He knows every circumstance that may lead you *away from* rather than *to* him. Identify those things that keep you from Him, and repent. Draw yourself back into His arms that are always open.

Chapter Four Notes

CHAPTER FIVE

Thyatira—The Tolerance Test

If you're like me, you sometimes wonder where things are going in our culture. "How do I say something? Is it right for me to say anything? If I say something will I offend someone?" The prophet Jeremiah said, "From the least to the greatest, all are greedy for gain; prophets and priests alike, all practice deceit" (Jeremiah 6:13 NIV).

Jeremiah rebuked the leaders of God's people, and it stung. All were missing the point—prophets and priests. Jeremiah continued to describe what these religious leaders had done that was so appalling to God: "They dress the wound of my people as though it were not serious. 'Peace, peace,' they say, when there is no peace. Are they ashamed of their detestable conduct? No, they have no shame at all; they do not even know how to blush" (Jeremiah 6:14–15 NIV).

God's people experienced no shame for their evil deeds; their consciences had become dulled to their corruption. Their attitude communicated, "As long as it's not hurting anybody else, it's okay." However, followers of Jesus must draw lines, regardless of how counter-culture this is. The plumb line of God's truth matters and makes a difference. Even Christians have become so focused on themselves that they have forgotten there is a divine moral framework that undergirds a healthy society.

Tolerance is held as the highest virtue today. The world worships tolerance because it doesn't want to offend anybody. Even legal systems attempt to keep people from offending.

Embracing tolerance births hyper-individualization. This mindset believes: "Everything is about me; therefore, if everything is about me, then the only thing that shouldn't be tolerated is something that affects me personally." Tolerance has become the fabric of American culture and has bred people who don't think beyond themselves. However, this goes against Jesus' teaching—He called people to love their neighbors as themselves (Mark 12:31).

What if a particular belief affects the cultural fabric of a nation, town, or community?

G. K. Chesterton, an English writer, philosopher, and theologian, said: "Tolerance is the virtue of a man without convictions."[55] But even those who trumpet tolerance will draw the line somewhere.

Everybody draws lines. The question is: Where, how, and what informs the line? It is paramount the right things are informing where believers draw their lines. If tolerance means condoning evil and injustice, we're in trouble, biblically speaking. Some draw the line at women's abuse issues, or perhaps kids shooting kids. They have drawn a line for what to them is right and wrong. But where will believers draw *their* lines?

What Is Tolerance?

One of my favorite speakers is Ravi Zacharias. He said, "Truth cannot be sacrificed at the altar of pretended tolerance. Real tolerance is deference for ideas and not indifference to the truth."[56]

I recently posted a question on Facebook that asked: When it comes to tolerance, where do you draw the line? Here are some responses I received:

- when it's dangerous
- when it becomes more than an annoyance, and it leaves your spirit with road rash
- when the evil becomes too great
- when you finally realize that tolerating was enabling
- when it breeds apathy and institutionalized discrimination
- when your agency is taken away
- when you are forced to accept others' beliefs as your own

Tolerance must go both ways, or it is not tolerance. True, healthy tolerance is about accepting folks where they are. Jesus was the perfect example of loving people regardless of political, religious, or cultural beliefs. He was tolerance in action and loved so much He was willing to point out sin. Unfortunately, the church is very good at replacing tolerant love with judgmental shaming, exhortation toward righteousness with enabling.

For me, because boundaries exist at the level of my core values but aren't hard-lines, they are contextual; if my values are threatened, I have to search myself to understand if another's actions will jeopardize the health and wellbeing of myself or others or is this my ego asserting itself? It might be that my tolerance of differences actually keeps me from being curious or open to learning.

Grace is something all believers can and should extend to all people, in all directions. Everyone is doing the best they can with what is available to them at this moment, myself included.

The City of Thyatira

Thyatira was not as big or wealthy as the other cities John addressed in Revelation. Thyatira was a smaller town in the middle of a valley on the road that connects Sardis with the capital, Pergamum. It was not strategic militarily, but a large garrison of troops was stationed there because it acted as a shield for the city of Pergamum. Any invading army heading toward the capital had to bypass Thyatira first, which effectively made this city collateral damage of any conflict in the region.[57] Invading armies would pause to thrash Thyatira while Pergamum bolstered its own defenses.

What Thyatira *did* boast was a strong trade system. Many guilds operated there.[58] Recall Paul's interaction with Lydia in Acts 16. Lydia was a seller of particular dyes, including a vibrant purple found in this region of the world. Lydia would have been a part of the flourishing guild system in Thyatira. Whatever the trade, whatever the business, there was a guild for it in Thyatira—though the predominant guilds were copper and bronze smelters. Trades went back for generations within families, so a baker likely followed in his father's footsteps—and probably their uncles and cousins did, too.

The guilds created a community, business, and religious experience that drove everything in the town of Thyatira. Sometimes visitors to this bustling trade center brought more than material wares, however; they exposed people to different beliefs, habits, and traditions.

The church of Thyatira, therefore, had both strengths and weaknesses and Jesus brought attention to both in Revelation 2. He said, "I know your works, your love and your faith and service and patient endurance, and that your latter works exceed the first" (Revelation 2:19 ESV).

Christ declared their love, faith, and patient endurance exceeded their works; this was the good news. A life embedded in the love of Jesus Christ ignites compassion which naturally results in service. Christians who don't serve are probably Christians who don't love, and a Christian who doesn't love needs to repent; likely they aren't aligned with what it means to be a Christian. The believer does not have the option to say, "Well, love isn't my gift. My gift is judgment." Followers of Jesus must embrace love as their core motivator because the God of love dwells within them. The desire to serve will be the natural overflow of that love.

So while the church at Thyatira seemed to be doing great things, Jesus told its members they might look holy and pure on the outside, but He knew what was really happening on the inside: "I have this against you," Jesus said, "that you tolerate the woman Jezebel, who calls herself a prophetess, and she teaches and leads My bond-servants astray so that they commit acts of immorality and eat things sacrificed to idols" (Revelation 2:20 NASB).

Apparently, this church was more tolerant than Jesus on certain issues; how apropos for society today.

Jezebel

Remember Jezebel, King Ahab's wife? Ahab was one of the worst kings in Israel's history. Jezebel was the daughter of the Phoenician king Ethbaal in Sidonia, which is in modern-day Lebanon. Jezebel worshipped Baal (the fertility god) and Asherah (the fertility goddess), and brought this worship into Israel when she married Ahab, thus slowly converting him.[59] Jezebel was terribly wicked: she set about destroying the prophets of Israel—for Israel did not worship any other gods—beginning with blending the religious systems.

Fast forward to Thyatira, whose city housed a prophetess with great influence and whom Jesus likened to Jezebel. This prophetess taught Jezebel's principles, which include sacred sexuality, sex with people other than one's spouse, and sacrificing to other gods.

Not only was this a problem for the church, but this Jezebel spirit also created problems for the entire culture. Recall Thyatira centered on the guild system. To feed one's family required participation in part of the trade union. Townspeople paid dues to join the guild, but each guild had its own god or goddess. Members attended guild meetings where they were required to worship pagan deities and sacrifice food to that guild's god. Then, by the end of the night, the meeting evolved into an enormous drunken orgy.

Christians, however, only worshipped one God—the God of Abraham, Isaac, and Jacob (see Deuteronomy 6:13, 10:20; Luke 4:8). Thus, they should not have been part of a guild—idol worship and sexual immorality were not acceptable behaviors for followers of Jesus. What were Christians living in Thyatira to do? The guilds were in control. The prophetess could have deceived Christians by saying: "God knows you need to feed your kids, so go to the guilds. Don't worry about it. God will forgive you."

Just like Balaam and the Nicolaitans, this prophetess mixed religions. She taught that God would extend forgiveness to Christians who worshipped pagan gods if it meant feeding their families.

Satan is an expert at dropping subtle temptations which in reality involve "cutting a deal with God." The result was Christians are divided in heart and mind. The apostle James called this being "double-minded," (James

1:8 NIV) and said, "Such people should not expect to receive anything from the Lord" (James 1:8 NLT).

However, this was where Jesus drew the line. When believers begin to cut deals with the enemy and compromise what God makes clear in Scripture, they cross that line. This is probably one of the biggest concerns in the church today. Christians don't want to affirm Jesus is the only way when the world says *everyone's* way is the right way. They shy away from making statements about what they believe to be true because other people who think differently may be offended. The line, however, was not written in erasable ink.

Jesus continued: "I have given her time to repent of her immorality, but she is unwilling. So I will cast her on a bed of suffering, and I will make those who commit adultery with her suffer intensely, unless they repent of her ways" (Revelation 2:21–22 NIV).

There are consequences for those who cross—or blur—that line.

When Should Christians Be Tolerant?

There is a difference between tolerance and acceptance. It is possible to be civically tolerant and respectful of others while drawing lines.

For example, particular systems, civil laws, and legal issues exist where tolerance must be practiced. There might be some laws Christians disagree with, and if so, they must work to change them to make a moral difference. However, this must be done with grace and truth as a guide.

This generation of Christians must also exert a level of social tolerance. A Christian may have Muslim, Hindu, Mormon, or Jehovah's Witnesses as neighbors. Each religion holds to different beliefs—according to the Bible, all are unbelievers. It's important that the Christian not expect them to act like believers when they are not. The Christian's belief system and moral framework are completely different as they adhere to the lines Scripture draws.

Christians also may have to exercise tolerance for other Christians who hold different theological beliefs. Some Christian churches believe in baptizing babies, while some teach only adults should be baptized. As long as both hold to the core primary truths of God, both are saved. When to baptize a person is a secondary issue; it is critical Christians employ tolerance with brothers and sisters who might believe differently. Some people believe in the gifts of the spirit, and some people speak in tongues while some believe the spiritual gifts ceased with the apostles. Those, too, are secondary issues.

So where are the lines of *intolerance*? When something happens in the church that is definitely off the scriptural mark—when a believer sins against another believer, for example—it cannot be ignored. In these situations, it is paramount believers enter into relational conversations and biblically contend with these issues. Matthew 18 provides details of how God orders this to be done:

If your brother or sister sins, go and point out their fault, just between just between the two of you. If they listen to you, you have won them over. But if they will not listen, take one or two others along, so that "every matter may be established by the testimony of two or three witnesses." If they still refuse to listen, tell it to the church; and if they refuse to listen even to the church, treat them as you would a pagan or a tax collector. **— Matthew 18:15–17 (NIV)**

In other words, when a brother or sister in Christ has sinned against you and needs correction, it should be done in a loving and relational way—not with a bullhorn or a picket sign. If they listen, praise God and move on. If they resist, the next step according to Matthew 18:15–17 is to bring in other witnesses. If they still refuse, it's time to bring the matter to church leadership.

In biblical times, some churches practiced shunning. They would bring a person to the platform, and if the person didn't repent, they'd boot him or her out of the church.[60] Unfortunately, some churches today continue this practice. This method breaks God's heart because it hurts and destroys relationships, making reconciliation even harder.

But God says there is a time and place to talk with someone who comes against Scripture. If a member of the church refuses to listen and receive the correction, they next should be released from the church. This does not mean other church members should stop loving them; on the contrary, they should extend grace to the person, but also hold to the understanding that God has drawn clear lines they have chosen to cross.

Everything is about grace; everything is about relationship. It's not about rules and checkboxes, but how Christians relate to each other when mistakes are made. Remember, truth cannot be sacrificed at the altar of pretended tolerance. With God's grace, differences can be accepted without comprising faith or relationships. Doing so will help guard the church today from falling into the same sins as the church at Thyatira.

Chapter Five Questions

Question: Have you grown tolerant of too many things in today's society? What do you tolerate that you shouldn't?

_____

_____

_____

_____

_____

_____

_____

_____

_____

_____

_____

Question: Where is your personal tolerance line? How did you know where to draw that line?

_____

_____

_____

_____

_____

_____

_____

_____

_____

_____

Question: What defines the difference between tolerance and acceptance for you?

_____

_____

_____

_____

_____

_____

_____

_____

_____

_____

Action: Jesus calls all Christians to love their neighbors. They are to extend grace to others, believers or not. Ask God to help you love others and extend His grace today.

Chapter Five Notes

_____

_____

_____

_____

_____

_____

_____

_____

_____

_____

_____

_____

_____

_____

_____

_____

_____

_____

_____

_____

CHAPTER SIX

Letting the Spirit Breathe

An unlikely group of persecuted men and women gathered in homes sprinkled throughout ancient Middle Eastern cities because they believed in a man who claimed to possess the words of life. This man, Jesus, called His followers to live differently, and pretty soon, these groups evolved into a fast-spreading movement. When an organism of people grows exponentially, systems must be created.

The book of Acts describes this movement. But as more and more people came to faith, some issues began to surface. In one case, Greek Jews complained against the Hebraic Jews because "their widows were being overlooked in the daily distribution of food" (Acts 6:1 NIV). Church leaders realized they needed structure to keep things in the church in order.

However, structure has the potential of killing the flow and movement of the Spirit which created the movement, to begin with. Without the Spirit, the movement risks becoming a machine that needs to be fed rather than an overflow of the life-giving Spirit which needs to be unleashed. If the Spirit is not allowed to lead, movements become monuments—edifices that stand for what the movement *used* to be. As more time passes, the monument is moved to a museum, and people pay a few bucks to look at what once was.

How can Christians free themselves in the midst of necessary systems? When churches become atrophied, they must revert to the basics: Jesus died for the sins of humanity, and people need to believe certain things to be His disciple. But if a person's understanding of the gospel stops with the theological proposition, they miss the entire point of why Jesus came.

Jesus did not come to help you:

- fulfill your dreams
- become a more moral person
- live your life safe and unaffected by the call of the gospel

Christians stand at the foot of the cross where Jesus said: "Follow me or don't." At the foot of the cross, those who profess faith in Jesus choose life while also choosing to put away the gods of materialism, commodities, and entertainment that occupy time, energy, and money. The church is not a country club; it's a mission. This becomes clear through Jesus' message to Sardis—a church that had, in fact, atrophied and become focused on materialism.

Waking Up Sardis

Sardis was likely the largest of all the churches because it had such a reputation. There was no persecution evident in the church of Sardis—no *thlipsis*. Somehow in Sardis, the church had become as tolerated as the Jewish synagogue in town. Sardis was one of the oldest cities in the region. There was a river in front of the city, and it was in this river the people of Sardis panned for gold[61]—which became the source of the city's and the church's wealth.

Interestingly, Sardis is also the Greek name for a stone. This stone surfaces later in the book of Revelation. About the best we can understand about the Sardis stone is that it is reddish in color[62] and that it is in the breastplate of high priests.[63] But it becomes such a commonplace stone that eventually it loses all its significance, much like the church.

This church has ancient roots. It is in an affluent area. It is also a strategic and militarily secure city. Sardis is a plural noun in the Greek, so there are actually two cities: one at the base of three mountains while at the top of the mountain lies the rest of the city.[64] This city was known to be impregnable—it was near impossible for enemies to take this city, except that they [were] besieged once when they [were] caught off guard and asleep.[65]

Jesus told this city, "Wake up! Strengthen what remains and is about to die, for I have found your deeds unfinished in the sight of my God" (Revelation 3:2 NIV).

It's time for the modern church to wake up as well. The body of Christ has been on autopilot, and the aftereffects are obvious. Christians have evolved to a place where they satiate their need to check off that "God" box. *I did my God duty. I read my Scripture. I went to church.* Yet that is not the dynamic relationship Jesus wants. That's energy, but there is no inward grace. Jesus says to the church today, "Wake up! Strengthen what remains."

Has your prayer life become dry and dutiful? Has your study of the Word of God become rote and ritual rather than life-giving? Has your service to those who are marginalized and needy become something you are doing out of habit, or do you have compassion in your soul?

Everything with Jesus is a movement. Mission happens not because of what believers do, but a result of the One who dwells within them. It is Christ that overflows, and the movement expands as a result of His compassion for people—not as a result of the believer's "duty." Religion is a duty. When was the last time you just let the Spirit move in you?

The One Problem with External Energy

The church at Sardis had become commonplace. In other words, it was no different than any other civic organization. There should be something radically different about believers who have the presence and the working of Jesus right in their midst. The church should look different from the world. The church at Sardis, however, had lost its significance. The church had become something that was tolerated.

The church at Sardis appeared to be doing everything right. They had "a reputation of being alive" (Revelation 3:1). However, Jesus knew what was really going on in the people's hearts. "I am looking under the hood, and you are dead," He reprimanded. Their external energy was not sufficient evidence of internal grace.

In American culture, good churches are often judged by external energy—by how large the building is, how many missionaries the church supports, or how full their parking lot is. None of these markers mean God's grace is alive and active in that church.

Believers should be able to walk into the smallest church and feel the Holy Spirit and worship, whether it's in collective silence, with hymns, or with a band.

Remembering

Remember, therefore, what you have received and heard; hold it fast, and repent. — ***Revelation 3:2 (NIV)***

Memories spark new life. Recall what it was like to be hungry for God, or a time when it seemed God answered every prayer. Perhaps somewhere along the way, you became spiritually dry, and said, "Well, maybe it's just a season," or "I guess maybe this is just the way God works." Instead of pressing in to Jesus and seeking His Word for new life, Christians often give in to the dry season, and it becomes normal.

Not only did Jesus call the church to remember, but He also told them to *watch* in Revelation 3:2. The phrase "wake up" and the word "watch" in the Greek is translated in the same way. Jesus says, "Watch!"

Well, what should believers be watching for?

False teachers. Peter wrote, "Your enemy the devil prowls around like a roaring lion looking for someone to devour" (1 Peter 5:8 NIV). There is spiritual warfare going on right now. If you don't think so, read the news. Look what's happening to the church. There is an enemy that wants to shut down the expression of the bride of Christ, and Christians should be praying for God's people—whether they are part of their tribe or not—because all people belong to God.

Temptation. On the night before Jesus was crucified, while praying in Gethsemane, He said, "Watch and pray so that you will not fall into temptation." (Matthew 26:41 NIV). Many find themselves caving to temptation, but God has given the presence of the Holy Spirit to all who have given their lives to Jesus. That means there is always time to call on the Holy Spirit to help you in the darkest hour before you take the drink, take the pill, or do the cutting. The Holy Spirit dwells within you so you can say, "I need you now." You have the body of Christ to be the living presence of Christ

Walking in Grace

A Christian's external energy—how they appear on the outside—isn't the evidence of powerful inward grace.

> *Yet you have still a few names in Sardis, people who have not soiled their garments, and they will walk with me in white, for they are worthy. The one who conquers will be clothed thus in white garments, and I will never blot his name out of the book of life. I will confess his name before my Father and before His angels.* — ***Revelation 3:4–5 (ESV)***

Enoch walked faithfully alongside God (Genesis 5:24). Often, when people walk together, one tells a story while the other listens. The two people learn about each other—they come to know each other better. The only distractions are things that distracted both parties.

Jesus said there were a few people in Sardis who "have not soiled their garments, and will walk with me in white."

Don't get lulled into sleep like some in Sardis—strive to be one of the "few names" who remain worthy. God wants you awake, alive, and aware. Those are the keys to abundant living, so "he who has an ear, let him hear what the Spirit says to the churches" (Revelation 3:6 ESV).

Chapter Six Questions

Question: How have you been on autopilot in your walk with God? Where do you need to wake up?

_____

_____

_____

_____

_____

_____

_____

_____

_____

_____

_____

Question: Have you walked with God lately, as Enoch walked—sharing stories and thoughts?

_____

_____

_____

_____

_____

_____

_____

_____

_____

_____

Question: When was the last time you can remember truly hungering for God?

_____

_____

_____

_____

_____

_____

_____

_____

_____

_____

Action: Jesus wants His people to wake up and walk with Him—closely, and focused. It is time to persevere and press into Him to rekindle the closeness you once had.

Chapter Six Notes

CHAPTER SEVEN

Brotherly Love—The Church at Philadelphia

If there is a church in the book of Revelation that the church today should strive to be like, it's the church in Philadelphia. Jesus loves and saturates a faithful church, a humble church, a believing church. These He infuses with His presence and grace and offers opportunities to share in the great commission of God.

How can the church influence and effect culture? How can the church *infect* culture when Christianity isn't the centerpiece? This message to the church in Philadelphia reveals how.

Philadelphia was the smallest of the seven churches, and also the youngest. The city only came into existence about 150 years before Christ.[66] It wasn't the most powerful or influential church, but according to Christ's words, it was the healthiest. Ancient Philadelphia is the modern-day Alaşehir, the city of God in modern-day Turkey. Philadelphia is located right between Laodicea and Sardis.[67] It was a border town, so the kingdom of Libya, the kingdom of Phrygia, and the kingdom of Mysia all converged in Philadelphia—making it what is called a cultural missional city. Philadelphia was established to infuse Greek culture in those other cities, and soon all were speaking Greek. Arts, culture, agriculture—it was all part of life in Philadelphia.

Unfortunately for the city, Philadelphia also was located in the middle of an area that experienced many earthquakes. The city suffered a massive earthquake in AD 17 that decimated the town of Philadelphia to rubble.[68]

Over time the city had three names. While Tiberius was on the throne, he paid to rebuild the city which was subsequently renamed Neo-Caesarea—the new city of Caesar—for a time. Sometime later while Vespasian (who had done some great things for the city) reigned, it was renamed Flavia after Vespasian's family name; eventually the name shifted back to Philadelphia. It was also known as the city of brotherly love and is actually named for its founders, two royal brothers, Attalus II and his brother, Eumenes.[69]

Philadelphia was the last city remaining after the Turkish and Islamist onslaught in that area starting in the 600s when Mohammed founded Islam. Afterward, it became a Christian city. All the other cities would fall under Turkish dominion. Twice Philadelphia would be besieged. When the Turkish and Byzantine armies gathered against Philadelphia, the church stood faithful right until the end. This was the last church to stand. God would keep their doors open for almost 1,400 years.[70]

The city is still booming to this day, and the church is still in use.

Holiness

To the angel of the church in Philadelphia write: the words of the holy one, the true one who has the key of David who opens and no one will shut and who shuts and no one will open. —Revelation 3:7 (ESV)

Jesus was called holy at His birth and holy at His death—His whole life was marked by holiness. The Greek word for holiness is *hágios* which means "to be different, to be set apart."[71] Jesus is fully human, but at the same time, He is different than any person. God is holy, and the Bible is clear that He is the only one who is really called holy. You need to understand that Jesus is starting by revealing his divinity again.

The presence of God is marked by holiness—a topic not spoken of often in twenty-first-century culture. Holiness is the absence of sin, the absence of anything broken, and the absence of a lack of peace. Holiness is purity, and something humans cannot fully experience on earth—and certainly cannot experience without God. The world is anything but holy.

Jesus said, "I am the holy one" in Revelation 3:7— clearly identifying Himself with God.

He also called Himself, "the true one." A Greek word for truth is *aléthinos*. Aléthinos means something is genuine or real.[72] Jesus was saying He is the genuine

One, the true One, affirming this throughout the New Testament. To His disciples Jesus said:

> *I am the way and the truth and the life. No one comes to the Father except through me.* —**John 14:16 (NIV)**

Now in Revelation 3, Jesus began to commend the Philadelphian church for what it had done right:

> *I know your deeds. See, I have placed before you an open door that no one can shut. I know that you have little strength, yet you have kept my word and have not denied my name.* — **Revelation 3:8 (NIV)**

The Philadelphian church probably took to heart everything James wrote in his letter, which declared, "Faith by itself, if it is not accompanied by action, is dead" (James 2:17 NIV). The natural response to belief in Christ and the understanding of what He did on the cross is action. Faith is more than information; it is more than correct doctrine and strong theology. Other churches boasted these characteristics—but Jesus still reprimanded them for lacking the presence of the living God.

> *I have set before you an open door, which no one is able to shut.* — **Revelation 3:8 (ESV)**

Jesus left what John called an open door to the Philadelphian church because of its faith. When a church is aligned with God, remaining in a constant state of confession and repentance before Jesus, it allows Him to lead. This was the characteristic Jesus praised in the church at Philadelphia. Thus, Jesus opens doors to share who He is—and as a result, believers become co-authors of new stories with God. This is so powerful!

Jesus next acknowledged the little power the Philadelphian church possessed:

> *I know you have but little power.* — **Revelation 3:8 (ESV)**

When a church or a person admits powerlessness, it opens the door for God's divine power to infuse them. God can use a willing person who is like a blank canvas. He fills them with His Spirit, and as the church expands, it is His glory that moves through His people; He is manifested. When the church relies on its power, it is likely to fall.

When you allow the God-given vocation He has placed on you and the light of Christ to live in you and illuminate through you, the world is changed.

In spite of their lack of power, the Philadelphian church did not deny Jesus' name and kept His word (Revelation 3:8 ESV). Recall John's words in his gospel which reveal what the Word is: "In the beginning was the Word, and the Word was with God, and the Word was God" (John 1:1 NIV). The Philadelphian church kept Jesus' teaching first and foremost, knowing He is the Word of God.

Everything Jesus taught culminates with just one command:

> *You shall love the Lord your God with all your heart and with all your soul and with all your mind. This is the great and first commandment. And a second is like it: You shall love your neighbor as yourself. On these two commandments depend all the Law and the Prophets.* **— Matthew 22:37–40 (ESV)**

Jesus taught the church to love—to love neighbors, friends, and enemies. The Philadelphian church understood this, and for that Jesus said, "You have not denied my name."

In spite of outside pressure they hadn't denied His name from a Jewish synagogue:

> *Behold, I will make those of the synagogue of Satan who say that they are Jews and are not, but lie— behold, I will make them come and bow down before your feet, and they will learn that I have loved you.* **— Revelation 3:9 (ESV)**

This Jewish synagogue condemned these gentile Christians for claiming Jesus was the fulfillment of the prophesied Messiah of the Hebrew Scriptures. Jesus used harsh words when describing these Jews, declaring they were "of the synagogue of Satan."

But back in Romans 9:6, Paul said there were those who are of Israel or in Israel but were not *of* Israel. In other words, a true Jew is one who honors the Lord as God. Just because a person's heritage is Jewish doesn't mean they are part of that remnant of believers. In the same way, a person can be in a church their whole life, but that doesn't make them a Christian.

Pillars for Philadelphia

I am coming soon. Hold fast what you have, so that no one may seize your crown. The one who conquers, I will make him a pillar in the temple of my God. Never shall he go out of it, and I will write on him the name of my God, and the name of the city of my God, the new Jerusalem, which comes down from my God out of heaven, and my own new name. He who has an ear, let him hear what the Spirit says to the churches. — **Revelation 3:11–13 (ESV)**

In the first century, when a person did something noteworthy in a city, their name was attached to pillars for people to view. The prophet Jeremiah foretold of a coming day when Israel's enemies would fight against her. In his prophecy, he referenced imagery of pillars where God said, "I make you this day a fortified city, an iron pillar ... they shall not prevail against you, for I am with you" (Jeremiah 1:18–19 ESV). In ancient times, pillars were pictures of strength, stability, and dignified beauty.

In Revelation 3:12, Jesus promised those who conquer (some translations say those who are victorious) will be made "a pillar in the temple of my God." God will make known to everyone, including the enemy, who His "pillars" are; He will write both the name of God and Jesus' new name on those faithful believers. These marks of identification will show who they belong to—the Lord.

In the first century, earthquakes were frequent—especially in Philadelphia. Often the only things left standing were the massive pillars. Jesus used this imagery to compare the Philadelphian believers to strong pillars that supported the church.

Finally, Jesus left the Philadelphian church with both a warning and a comfort: He is returning! "I am coming soon," He declared in Revelation 3:11. For those who are ready, Jesus' return as King of Kings and Lord of Lords is a great comfort and the hope they cling to (Hebrews 6:18). However, for those who aren't prepared for Jesus to come soon—it's a somber warning.

WORKBOOK

Chapter Seven Questions

Question: Where in your life do you see holiness? What does "holy" mean to you?

_____

_____

_____

_____

_____

_____

_____

_____

_____

_____

Question: What situations in your life have left you feeling powerless? Have you invited God into them?

_____

_____

_____

_____

_____

_____

_____

_____

_____

_____

Question: How are you serving others?

_____

_____

_____

_____

_____

_____

_____

_____

_____

_____

_____

Action: If Jesus is coming soon, believers need to walk in His power and serve His people. He alone is holy, and holiness is desperately needed in this world. Seek His holy hand in your life today.

Chapter Seven Notes

CHAPTER EIGHT

The Pride of Laodicea

A road from Ephesus led straight up to Laodicea, ascending about 8,500 feet. Upon arriving at the top, the gates of Phrygia opened to the city of Laodicea. It was a wealthy area, stationed on all of the crossroads. Trade was prevalent as Laodicea sat at the marketing epicenter for the entire region. When Revelation was written, Laodicea was probably three hundred years old.[73]

With excessive wealth comes the possibility of increased pride. The Laodiceans possessed a great deal of pride in several areas.

Their Wealth

Laodicea was the region's financial center and Cicero did his banking there.[74] Wealth brings enterprise, which created a culture of high income for people all throughout the city. The historian Tacitus noted

Laodicea in his book *The Annals*: "This is one of the most famous cities of Asia."

At one point, Laodicea and several other cities were leveled by an earthquake. But Tacitus wrote that "in the same year, they were overthrown by an earthquake and without any relief from us [the Roman government] ... it rebuilt itself."[75] When a severe hurricane like Katrina or Harvey wreaks destruction through a city, could you imagine the mayor saying to FEMA, "No thank you. We want no financial assistance. We will rebuild this city out of our wealth"?

The prideful city of Laodicea essentially communicated this to Rome: "We're good. Quite frankly, we're wealthier than you. We don't need help." And it was true! The Laodiceans rebuilt their city—though eventually it was completely decimated by another earthquake.

Their Affluent Style

Laodicea was known for an ultra-soft, shiny violet-black wool.[76] It was a luxurious item; clothing made from the wool of Laodicea communicated a person was wealthy. The Laodiceans were proud of their affluence, which was reflected in their clothing.

Their Medical Center

A homeopathic medical center in Laodicea provided an ointment as a salve to help people with eye and ear problems.[77] People came from far and wide to trade and purchase these and other products in hopes of finding healing in this city.

The Real Amen

*To the angel of the church of Laodicea, write: "These are the words of the Amen, the faithful and true witness, the ruler of God's creation." — **Revelation 3:14 (NIV)***

Jesus described Himself in Revelation 3:14 and revealed who He is and His sovereign connection to God: He is the Amen, the faithful and true witness, the ruler of God's creation. The word "amen" in Hebrew means "firm" or "faithful."[78] Jesus is completely true and entirely trustworthy. In those days, when someone spoke truth, others would affirm its truth by saying, "Amen." It was similar to saying, "I receive it," or "Make it so—I am in agreement with that."

In Revelation 3:14, Jesus pronounced He is one hundred percent true and trustworthy. He is *the* "Amen."

I have many pictures of my wife. When I look at her picture, I can affirm, "Oh! That's my wife, that's Amy. I recognize her by the picture."

When you've seen Jesus, you have seen God. Jesus is the snapshot, the picture the Divine has given humanity so that people know how God loves, works amongst His people, disciplines those He loves, and empowers believers.

Jesus is the image of the invisible God (Colossians 1:15), the firstborn, the beginning of all creation. The apostle Paul wrote:

> *For by Him all things were created, both in the heavens and on earth, visible and invisible, whether thrones or dominions or rulers or authorities—all things have been created through Him and for Him. He is before all things, and in Him all things hold together.* — ***Colossians 1:16–17 (NLT)***

Jesus is the cosmic energy force that holds the stars, gravity, planets, and universes in place. Jesus is not only a man who walked the earth 2,000 years ago and taught a few good ideas that are wise to follow; He is God in the flesh.

When you see Jesus, you've finally seen God. He's the foundation of creation; He's the Genesis, the beginning. All things came into being through Him, and every person who puts their faith in Jesus becomes a part of Him.

The Fatal Flaw

When Jesus described Himself in Revelation 3:14, He spoke truth to a church that needed to hear those specifics of who He is. Imagine speaking to an ultra-prideful church or community that thinks it is the genesis of everything; when the Laodiceans heard this message, they were likely shaken up. Recall the Laodiceans did not want help from anyone or any government—and this they don't need God. They possess many things—cash, capacity, education—but at the end of the day, they believe they know more than God. This hyper-individualization of culture disconnects people from each other and from God. Ultimately, it creates a system and structure that keeps God on the outside of everything they do because they believe they are self-sufficient.

Phrases like, "I pulled myself up by the bootstraps," "I can do this," and "I don't need any help" reflect this innate desire to be self-sufficient. Do you struggle with asking for help from other people? This is a broken part of people's cultural DNA, and something they actually need to repent of. Hyper-individualization evolves quickly to materialism which is focused on self.

People choose a church based on whether it has the kind of music they like, a facility they like, and a kids' program that works for them. Everything in American culture, even a person's spirituality, is about "how does this work best for me?" not "where is God calling me to connect with the community in faith and give my life away?"

In the first century, there was only one church in each city (and not yet in every city) a person could attend if they were a Christian. If they didn't like it, they had no alternative option. No one had a choice about the speaker, the music, or the kids' program; the carpet color didn't matter, nor the lights, and there was certainly no PowerPoint to help believers stay focused on the message. When the church gathered, the focus was on the living presence of Jesus Christ manifesting in that place to transform believers' lives so that the kingdom of

WORKBOOK

Chapter Eight Questions

Question: How are you like the city of Laodicea? What are you the most prideful about?

_____

_____

_____

_____

_____

_____

_____

_____

_____

_____

_____

_____

Question: How does society reflect self-sufficiency—and no need for God?

_____

_____

_____

_____

_____

_____

_____

_____

_____

_____

Question: Are you lukewarm in your love of God? How can you rekindle the fire in your soul?

_____

_____

_____

_____

_____

_____

_____

_____

_____

_____

_____

Action: Now is the time to lay your pride at Jesus' feet and accept your true need of Him. He is the Amen—the picture of God for you to follow. Commit to follow His leading today.

Chapter Eight Notes

CHAPTER NINE

Understanding Right Worship

How can that which is utterly indescribable be described? Einstein said:

> I'm not an atheist, and I don't think I can call myself a pantheist. We are in the position of a little child entering a huge library filled with books in many languages. The child knows someone must have written those books. It does not know how. It does not understand the languages in which they are written. The child dimly suspects a mysterious order in the arrangement of the books but doesn't know what it is. That, it seems to me, is the attitude of even the most intelligent human being toward God. We see the universe marvelously arranged and obeying certain laws but only dimly understand these laws.[81]

Christians, too, may experience this partial understanding of God, and then they begin to see life and God so much differently when they understand worship. It's therefore, no coincidence the core issue for these seven churches Jesus addressed in Revelation was a lack of right worship.

"After this I looked, and there before me was a door," John said in Revelation 4:1 (NIV). Somehow Jesus becomes a divine portal. Remember, He called Himself "The gate" or the "door" (John 10:9) and "the way" (John 14:6). He is a door into a whole other realm.

Thin Spaces

In Celtic Christianity, thin spaces are those moments in life when the presence and experience of God are so tangible that the veil between heaven and earth is removed and you sense God.[82] For example, when a community of faith (a church body) gathers and prepares for the intention of meeting God, Celtic Christianity teaches believers walk into this thin space.

John described an opening to a different realm in his vision, saying, "After this I looked, and behold, a door standing open in heaven!" (Revelation 4:1 ESV). Most think he looked up to see a strange door that opened up while he gazed through it, rather than a portal right next to him; this is because Jesus said the kingdom of God is in the believer's midst; it is all around the church (Luke 17:21). Regardless, Jesus is the door to something human beings can only speculate about.

Some people interpret Revelation 4 as evidence of the rapture of the church—they believe the church is now in heaven. John was not describing the rapture, but rather, worship. Time is part of the created order. The same way elephants, water, rocks, and minerals are part of the created order, and the same way human beings are also a part of this order, so is time. Time did not exist until God created the universe, and human beings don't understand time well. The moon, sun, and earth generate a measurement of movement—thus, time only exists because of those things God created.

The elements are how time is charted and measured. Before that, God has always existed beyond time and space. Revelation 4 and 5 describe John stepping into the "eternal present," where eternity past, present, and future are all held together in God who is called the Eternal One.

God is spirit. He doesn't age; He doesn't change. He can't be marked by time. God is moving time toward the ultimate victory in the Bible—the victory over death. When there is no more death, there will be no more time. At this point, there will be no more sun because the presence of God will become the sun. The sun will no longer mark time, as the earth will no longer orbit around the sun. Revelation is clearly more than a story about a raptured church.

What do believers do when the church tries to determine what and how they worship? What do believers do when the church has lost its way, compromised beliefs, and succumbed to worldly influences?

When the church is no longer hot nor cold, no longer therapeutic nor refreshing to the community or world, what are God's people to do?

When the church has fallen asleep, thinking it is on track when, in fact, God says it is dead, what should believers do?

Worship.

When the church is dead, believers need to look into the center of God's throne room, and there they will find something unique.

The Indescribable Majesty and Presence

When the veil between human reality and the ever-present spiritual reality is removed, the resonating hum at the center of the universe is revealed: worship. A divine song of beauty declaring the holiness and worthiness of God dwells in colored light beyond description. Using human words, John tried to describe what he saw, beginning with the sound of a voice:

> *And the voice I had first heard speaking to me like a trumpet said, "Come up here, and I will show you what must take place after this." — **Revelation 4:1 (NIV)***

John was about to enter into everything—past, present, and future—all from his view at that thin space revealing to him that worship is a response to Jesus.

In this current tangible kingdom on earth, worship is a response to the primary or the first movements of God. People produce nothing original in and of themselves; they don't randomly decide to walk in a church on a given Sunday. Rather, that "drawing" toward God is a response to something God has previously done. When God moves, people respond in worship. In Revelation 4:1, Jesus invited John to "come up here," and John responded. When a person responds to God, it is always as a secondary movement to the primary cause who is God.

John described what he saw next: "Around the throne were twenty-four thrones, and seated on the thrones were twenty-four elders, clothed in white garments with golden crowns on their heads" (Revelation 4:4 ESV). At the center of God's throne room, John saw worship.

How could John describe something that's indescribable? John used the phrase, "I looked" in this letter seventy times and, "I heard" thirty-five times. This isn't theology, but John's honest experience, and it's absolutely beautiful.

There is a peculiar occurrence that many share who have had a life-after-death experience; they describe an incredible light. Whether they saw something similar to John is impossible to know; however, it is clear from God's Word that God is this incredible, unapproachable, utterly amazing light in Revelation 4. John moved through the veil between the physical and the supernatural to this "light."

In July 2010, Paul Crowther, Professor of Astrophysics from the University of Sheffield's Department of Physics and Astronomy, announced he and his research team had discovered a star they described as the biggest star ever found in the universe. Not even a welder's helmet would help you face the light from this giant star.[83] The mass of the star is roughly

265 times that of the sun. But that's nothing: the star's brightness is some ten million times greater than the light coming from the sun. The star is named R136A1.[84] It's not twice as bright as the sun; rather, this newly identified star is ten million times brighter than the sun.

How can anything be that bright? And yet *it pales in comparison to God.*

John described the throne surrounded by twenty-four elders, clothed in white garments with golden crowns on their heads (Revelation 4:4 ESV). It is not clear who the twenty-four elders are, although there are many theories. Some think it's the compilation in heaven of the twelve patriarchs in the Old Covenant, and the twelve Apostles in the New—representing all believing saints for all of eternity. Other people think the elders are "super-angels" who lead worship.

Jesus said in the gospel of Matthew that the twelve apostles would sit on thrones. Some critics have countered the "real" heaven isn't completely in place yet, so there isn't a human in heaven other than Jesus. Yet Paul said to be absent from the body is to be present with the Lord (2 Corinthians 5:8). According to Paul, upon death, a believer is immediately with Christ.

Regardless of personal interpretation, these elders were clothed in white, signifying purity, with golden crowns on their heads. The Bible speaks of a number of different crowns: the crown of righteousness, the crown of perseverance, the crown of life—all of which connect to rewards believers will receive one day for faithfully following and aligning with the Lord.

Then John proclaimed:

From the throne came flashes of lightning, and rumblings and peals of thunder, and before the thrones were burning seven torches of fire, which are the seven spirits of God, and before the throne there was as it were a sea of glass, like crystal. — **Revelation 4:5–6 (ESV)**

His Majesty

John's description of the throne room presented an image of worship that focused on the majesty of God. Majesty is not a word often used in modern-day vernacular. But with the word comes respect, reverence, a sense of awe, and a little tentativeness. Sometimes it's easy to make Jesus like a buddy and forget He is absolutely holy.

This imagery also speaks to His mystery. Worship is clandestine, and trying to make sense of every doctrine, every theology, and every element of a text robs God of His mystery. John doesn't try to put the supernatural into super-tangible terms; there are things in the eternal that are simply *intangible* and will remain a mystery this side of heaven.

As Einstein commented, "The most beautiful thing we can experience is the mysterious. It is the source of all true art true science. He to whom this emotion is a stranger, who can no longer pause to wonder and stand rapt in awe, is as good as dead: his eyes are closed. This insight into the mystery of life, coupled though it be with fear, has also given rise to religion. To know that what is impenetrable to us really exists, manifesting itself as the highest wisdom and the most radiant beauty which our dull faculties can comprehend only in their most primitive forms—this knowledge, this feeling, is at the center of true religiousness. In this sense, and in this sense only, I am a devoutly religious man."[85]

God's Deserving Throne

What John clearly communicated to that generation and culture was clear: *Domitian was not on the heavenly throne.*

The One at the center of all things, the One at the center of the universe where the hum is always flowing—He is the One who sits upon the ultimate throne. Man-made thrones can be toppled by God at any moment. A church under pressure and struggling, or being crushed by the established government, needs only to worship the One who is over those kings and human leaders. John addressed the believers' concern of Domitian snuffing them out, reminding them there's a King who is sovereign, who is full of beauty and full of mystery, and who is enshrouded in majesty and purity. The white robes, the golden crowns—everything spoke of holiness and beauty and purity.

John continued, describing heaven's throne room:

> *Before the throne there was as it were a sea of glass, like crystal. And around the throne, on each side of the throne, are four living creatures, full of eyes in front and behind: the first living creature like a lion, the second living creature like an ox, the third living creature with the face of a man, and the fourth living creature like an eagle in flight. And the four living*

creatures, each of them with six wings, are full of eyes all around and within, and day and night they never cease to say, "Holy, holy, holy, is the Lord God Almighty, who was and is and is to come!" — **Revelation 4:6–8 (ESV)**

It is easy to try and interpret these verses by focusing on the symbolism of the imagery—but John's message was much simpler. Worship includes all of God's creation, not just mortals. God created everything. Remember, Jesus said even the rocks would cry out if God's people don't (Luke 19:40).

Christianity is a singing faith. In the midst of singing, God displays His presence and power in a profound way—especially in the corporate body of Christ. Worship through song realigns believers with God's holiness and beauty. When living creatures give glory, honor, and thanks to Him who is seated on the throne and lives forever and ever, the twenty-four elders fall down before Him as well and cast their crowns before the throne. All they have earned is worthless when they finally see God face to face: "Worthy are you, our Lord and God, to receive glory honor and power, for you created all things, and by your will they existed and were created" (Revelation 4:11 ESV).

Christian author Richard Foster wrote: "Just as worship begins in holy expectancy, it ends in holy obedience ... Holy obedience saves worship from becoming an opiate, an escape from the pressing needs of modern life."[86] Worship reflects the light of God and infuses believers with His presence in a way that then turns His rays and displays His ways to the world. So what would we need to do as we worship again? When you don't feel like worshiping; it's probably the right time to worship.

Worship is a thin space. Wherever you go—whether riding the metro to Seattle to go to work, driving a car, coaching Little League, or sitting in a coffee shop—you have the opportunity to step into that thin space and sing the song that is the hum of the universe. Jesus invites you to come boldly—not terrified, not afraid, but boldly—because in Christ, you are clean, forgiven, and graced. You have received His mercy, and you have the opportunity to experience the God who was once unapproachable. Embrace this, and move through the thin space of worship.

Chapter Nine Questions

Question: What was the last time you remember being in a "thin space"? How did it feel?

_____

_____

_____

_____

_____

_____

_____

_____

_____

_____

Question: How does worship remove the veil between reality on earth and heaven?

_____

_____

_____

_____

_____

_____

_____

_____

_____

_____

Question: How can you worship God in every area of your life?

_____

_____

_____

_____

_____

_____

_____

_____

_____

_____

_____

_____

Action: God is continually welcoming believers into a thin space. It is their job to reach through the veil and let their soul hum with the song worship it was designed to sing. God is eternally there, waiting to reach back.

Chapter Nine Notes

CHAPTER TEN

Worship Unleashed

Song is at the heartbeat of everything in the mission of God. Eugene Peterson wrote, "In worship, we cease being predators who by stealth approach everyone as prey that we can pull in to our center. We respond to the center. We are privileged listeners and respondents who offer ourselves to God who creates and redeems."[87]

Peterson wrote that many a congregation assembling in a church must look to the angels like a muddy, puddle-strewn shore at low tide, littered with every kind of rubbish and odds and ends—a distressing sort of spectacle—and then the tide of worship comes in, and it's all gone. The cleansing sea flows over the whole lot, so God's people are released from a narrow, selfish outlook on the universe by a common act of worship.

As the worship of God moves over a congregation and then flows back out, it washes, cleanses, purifies, and beautifies every negative thing people bring that creates the spectacle.

Unsealing the Scroll

Consider what John saw and heard next:

Because then I saw in the right hand of him who sat on the throne a scroll with writing on both sides and sealed with seven seals. And I saw a mighty angel proclaiming in a loud voice, "Who is worthy to break the seals and open the scroll?" — **Revelation 5:1–2 (NIV)**

The scroll John described would have been nearly fifteen feet in length. Most scrolls had writing on only one side—the smooth side with horizontal fibers. The other side's fibers were vertical and thus went against the grain making it difficult for writing. Rarely did a scroll exist with writing on both sides unless it was a legal document. When John saw the scroll in Revelation 5:1–2 with writing on both sides, he knew it had something to do with the authority of God.

An ancient scroll would have been bound with pieces of wax sealing the scroll, which would have been impressed with a signet ring. Signet rings were like the personal signature of the only person legally able to open the scroll. If your ring matched the impression in the wax seal, you were the rightful owner of the scroll, and you alone had the legal capacity to open it.[88]

In John's vision, he saw a scroll with seven seals. The scroll contained God's mission—His plan for the redemption of the universe, the plan He would institute so that all people could walk into His throne room. This plan looks back to the beginning in Genesis when it was enacted.

The angel in Revelation 5:1–2 asked: Who has legal authority to open the scroll?

The first thing some people in the seven churches likely noticed was that even Domitian did not have authority to open this scroll. There was no king, ruler, or person so holy or so perfect they could rightfully open this heavenly scroll. Who in the household of Adam could possibly be the one worthy of opening the scroll?

John began to weep because there was no one worthy.

But wait! John continued with good news:

> *Behold, the Lion of the tribe of Judah, the Root of David, has conquered, so that he can open the scroll and its seven seals.* **—Revelation 5:5 (NIV)**

There is One in the household of Adam who has the capacity and worthiness—the signet ring—to match the seven seals and open this scroll and thus bring about the fullness of the rule and reign of God. There is One who can right every wrong, overcome every injustice, and push back oppression. There is one person who can open the scroll—the Lion of the tribe of Judah, the root of David.

Jesus has authority to open the double-sided scroll!

John was describing something radical happening in heaven, and it was not a rock concert. The mission of God was being unfolded as all in heaven worshipped.

This heavenly reality is energetic, active, moving, and empowered.

Lion or Lamb?

And between the throne and the four living creatures and among the elders I saw a Lamb standing, as though it had been slain. **— Revelation 5:6 ESV**

Does something about the phrasing of this verse in Revelation 5:6 seem off? If something had been slain—and the Greek word, *sphazō,* is actually "slaughtered"[89]—the creature would generally not be doing well.

Imagine John watching and waiting to see this massive Lion of Judah. He turns to see the Warrior, the proud One, the King, the sovereign One, but he understands too He is the slaughtered Lamb of God. The victory by the Lion is accomplished through the Lamb. The church has been trying to win the world by being like a lion but would do better resembling the Lamb. The world needs to encounter the Lamb's grace, meekness, and beauty.

The Lamb was standing, according to John, "with seven horns and with seven eyes" (Revelation 5:6 ESV). Seven is the number for completeness. Seven horns indicate power and authority,[90] so this image is not merely a peculiar lamb with horns. Rather, this slain Lamb, the sacrificial One, had all power and all authority.

All the Bowed Knees

And he went and took the scroll from the right hand of him who was seated on the throne. **— Revelation 5:7 ESV**

The Greek word for "seated" in Revelation 5:7 is *kathémai*. Kathémai means enthroned, as a king sits on his throne, or to dwell or reside.[91] God dwells on His throne and invites us to worship Him there.

Unfortunately, the West holds a limited view of what worship is. Often worship is defined as the time in church where a band leads a few songs about God. While that is *part* of worship, that is not *all* that worship involves. Worshipping Jesus starts by living a life with a worship mentality, one where all a person does is seeking to bring glory to the King.

When a believer lifts their whole being to the Lord in prayer, in song, in service, and in worship, they will find themselves in the throne room of heaven, approaching God where he dwells.

Do you ever wonder if God listens? Does He care about the details of your life? In John's vision, the prayers of the saints fill golden bowls, described as "full of incense" (Revelation 5:8 ESV). Yes, God hears.

Believers' prayers ascend before the throne of God; He hears every single request, cry, and praise—and He moves. Every prayer, every pain, and every tear becomes a part of what God is doing in the midst of the earth because God's mission is fueled by His people's worship and prayer.

His Worthiness

Why is Jesus the worthy one? Because He was slain, He gave his life, He gave His blood, and He ransomed God's people from every nationality, race, language, and culture. All are called into one kingdom regardless of where they live.

He is worthy because He gave His life. In Revelation 5, John referenced Exodus with the imagery of the Passover lamb by whose blood the firstborn sons of Israel were saved from death. In this vision, God is gathering all people from every nation and making them into a brand-new community, or a kingdom of priests.

Jesus came to create a kingdom in which all people worship God, have access to God, and serve as priests in this new community. Those who believe are part of the mission which flows from worship; together they will reign with Him on the earth. Their voices co-mingle with angels' voices!

Then I looked, and I heard around the throne and the living creatures and the elders the voice of many angels, numbering myriads of myriads and thousands of thousands, saying with a loud voice, "Worthy is the Lamb who was slain, to receive [seven things, including] power and wealth and wisdom and might and honor and glory and blessing!" — **Revelation 5:11–12 (ESV)**

The church needs to reclaim what it was saved from and placed on a mission for, which is to live a life of worship. When the church's mission flows from worship, when it flows from a place aligned with God, everything is different. Scripture is clear those who heard John's message in the seven churches knew only God received praise, glory, and honor; thus, in Revelation 5:11–12, John was describing the enthronement of Jesus as God.

This changes things.

Jesus isn't just a great teacher who died for you. He is God in human flesh who came to rescue you, redeem you, restore you, and set you in the midst of a community of faith so that you can worship and bring about the illumination of Jesus thereby fulfilling God's great mission as the scrolls are unsealed.

Everything should flow from worship. If the church became a fellowship of worshipers, everything God's people would do would illuminate the One—the Lamb who is the Lion. Jesus, the Root of David who is at the center of the universe, would rightly receive all glory, honor, and praise.

Chapter Ten Questions

Question: What reassurance can you embrace knowing God hears your prayers and moves on them?

_____

_____

_____

_____

_____

_____

_____

_____

_____

_____

Question: At the core of everything, what is your mission on the earth?

_____

_____

_____

_____

_____

_____

_____

_____

_____

_____

Question: What makes Jesus worthy to you?

_____

_____

_____

_____

_____

_____

_____

_____

_____

_____

_____

Action: Reclaim your mission that Jesus died for. Accept your life's mission of worship and watch your life and others' lives change.

Chapter Ten Notes

CHAPTER ELEVEN

Hope in Darkness

People are angry. They argue on the radio, quarrel on TV—they even squabble over Tweets and status updates; clearly, the world is experiencing a lot of pain, the root of anger. There are no simple answers, but when something distressing happens, people polarize. It drives them to ask: What in the world is going on?

When assault hits every level of morality, people look around for who to blame. Why? It is because they hold a false belief that blaming someone else will resolve the problem and ease the pain quicker. They're stumbling toward light, hoping it offers a reprieve.

People are looking for hope in the wrong place. In his phenomenal book *A Grace Disguised: How the Soul Grows Through Loss,* Jerry Sittser wrote: "The quickest way for anyone to reach the sun and the light of day is not to run west chasing after the setting sun but to head east plunging into the darkness until one comes to the sunrise."[92] Rather than running toward good, people run to evil—thinking it is good.

In Revelation, Christ reveals true hope is found only in Him; the book reveals Jesus has answers to the four greatest plights of humanity through the narratives of conquest, violence, poverty, and death.

The Breaking of the Seals

The next chapters of Revelation do not necessarily describe what is to come, but rather what has already taken place (There are some things yet to come, but quite different from the uniquely Americanized version of *Left Behind*).

John watched as the only one who was able opened a seal:

> *Now I watched when the Lamb opened one of the seven seals. — **Revelation 6:1a (ESV)***

The early church believed that as soon as Jesus ascended to heaven and went back to the Father, the tribulation period had begun. In fact, the generation that came after Jesus had witnessed the destruction of Jerusalem in AD 70,[93] a horrific event Jesus spoke about in Revelation 6.

The Four Horsemen of the Apocalypse

> *And I heard one of the four living creatures say with a voice like thunder, "Come!" And I looked, and behold,*

*a white horse! And its rider had a bow, and a crown was given to him, and he came out conquering, and to conquer. — **Revelation 6:1b–2 (ESV)***

John first described a white horse hell-bent on conquering reminiscent of Job; God had given Satan some leeway to try and push Job toward denouncing God.

What was unleashed and what God allowed into the world was *conquest*. With a bow, a crown, and a white horse, hearers of the message were given the perfect biblical image of a winner. It fit culturally, too: after sacking another nation, Rome would take chariots led by white horses and wear their crowns and white robes and ride through the town proclaiming their victory over those whom they had just defeated.[94]

The Old Testament often presents imagery of weapons called "bows." When Israel was conquering an enemy, they were to break and give up their bows,[95] and the Parthians (Rome's one major enemy) rode white horses well-equipped with bows. Roman citizens who heard the contents of John's letter would have recognized this imagery; they knew the bow meant a takeover.

The word conquering in Revelation 6:2 would have brought to mind images of armies crossing borders to subjugate and defeat enemies. Thus, the rider on the white horse *is a man of conquest.*

Next, John described another horse, this time one that was bright red:

> *When he opened the second seal, I heard the second living creature say, "Come!" And out came another horse bright red. Its rider was permitted to take peace from the earth, so that people should slay one another, and he was given a great sword.* — **Revelation 6:3–4 (ESV)**

Along with a red horse, John described a "great sword" (Revelation 6:4) indicative of war. The rider on the red horse was described as removing peace from the earth which led to people slaying each other. God allowed this war in John's vision, as well as the subsequent conflict and violence.

In John's vision, the red horse removed all superficial peace people pretend to create. With a mindset focused on conquest, the inevitable reality or outplay is always war and violence; it is impossible to separate the two.

It is by God's grace that He works within man's perverted norms, as people seem to have an unfortunate fascination with violence, war, and death. It's on television shows, in the movies, and most pronounced in video games. This generation's egos chase after the adrenaline rush that comes from watching or participating in these dark things. People are seen as things to be bartered with in violence—a frightening concept.

It is paramount that Christians bring darkness into the light of reality. Violence, pain, and addiction must be dealt with! If you are in denial of a habit or a hang-up and keeping it secret, you will never get healthy from it.

A conquering mindset involves confronting systemic issues in modern culture by bringing those issues out into the open. Through John's vision, God is showing His people what is so wrong and why the world so desperately needs Him.

Wheat for a Denarius

> *When the Lamb opened the third seal, I heard the third living creature say, "Come!" I looked, and there before me was a black horse! Its rider was holding a pair of scales in his hand. Then I heard what sounded like a voice among the four living creatures, saying, "Two pounds of wheat for a day's wages, and six pounds of barley for a day's wages, and do not damage the oil and the wine!" — **Revelation 6:5–6 (NIV)***

Here John described a conquest that lead to violence and war, a famine, and ultimately economic collapse. When an economic collapse happens, war is good for some segments of society and not good for others. It may be good for the financially well-off, but disastrous for those struggling to make ends meet. The black horse embodies a number of societal woes that placed people in need of rescue: inequality, injustice, poverty, and famine.

During war, Domitian would command his soldiers to destroy the wheat fields knowing that in about a year, those fields would come back. However, they did not tend to destroy grapevines or olive trees, because regrowth took much longer. If it was going to take more than twenty years to receive a return on something that produced a valuable commodity, the conquering military would leave it alone.

The cost John mentioned, "Two pounds of wheat for a day's wages, and six pounds of barley for a day's wages" (Revelation 6:6), was enough wheat to feed only one person in a family. These prices were about fifteen times the normal price of wheat and barley during this time— indicating steep inflation that would make it incredibly difficult for poor people to buy even a loaf of bread. Conquest and violence generally hurt the underprivileged far more than they hurt the rich.

Americans tend to say "What about the problems on our soil?" They are so insulated in comfort they don't realize the poor in this country are rich by comparison. The poorest Americans are rich when compared to the rest of the world. Have followers of Christ plugged their ears to the cries of their brothers and sisters all over the world?

Needing God

*When he opened the fourth seal, I heard the voice of the fourth living creature saying, "Come and see." So I looked and behold, a pale horse. And the name of him who sat on it was Death, and Hades followed with him. And power was given to them over a fourth of the earth, to kill with the sword, with hunger, with death, and by the beasts of the earth. — **Revelation 6:7–8 (NKJV)***

Cloros is the Greek word for the English word "pale." This paleness John referred to was a pale green sickliness.[96]

Every year under Domitian's reign, this evil ruler would initiate the Domitian games—similar to the early Olympics, but to honor Domitian, who was clearly quite full of himself.[97] The games were a spectacle for watching Christians be executed for entertainment, though some non-Christians were killed as well at these gladiatorial events.

The followers of Christ who read John's letter, or listened to it being read, were well aware of what transpired at the Domitian games. The image of four different-colored horses (Revelation 6:1–8) would have reminded early Christians of the races between horses from four factions represented by different colors. And the image of Hades following the fourth horseman, bringer of death, doubtless evoked the man wearing a Hades mask who removed the dead bodies from the arena at the end of the games.[98]

God has an "upper story" that will one day eliminate the reality of what happened at the games. He operates in both a sovereign "upper story" as well as in an earthly, day-to-day "lower story." His upper story is always at work moving history toward its perfect ending. However, we experience the mystery and pain of the daily lower story, which often makes no sense.

One day, the fulfillment of God's plan and purpose will bring healing to what was experienced in the lower story of Domitian's games, and to your current struggle.

But at that moment, Christians were living out their lower story. Thus, the fourth pale horse signified death.

In spite of the devastating events described above, Jesus is in control even when circumstances are painful. God has limited the scope of each of the four rider's abilities. They have permission to do some things that reveal humanity's great need for God, but they will always be under God's sovereign rule. This is not unlike how Satan could not do anything more to Job than what God allowed.

In the next scene, John described something profound—that connects to believers today.

> *When he opened the fifth seal, I saw under the altar the souls of those who had been slain because of the word of God and the testimony they had maintained. They called out in a loud voice, "How long, Sovereign Lord, holy and true, until you judge the inhabitants of the earth and avenge our blood?"* — ***Revelation 6:9–10 (NIV)***

Martyrs under God's altar cry out, "How long ... until you judge the inhabitants of the earth?" in Revelation 6:10. This is imagery drawn from Leviticus 4:7 which says, "The rest of the bull's blood he shall pour out at the base of the altar of burnt offering at the entrance to the tent of meeting" (NIV). God will one day set everything right; those who have persecuted God's people will be judged.[99] Without skipping a beat, John next described a coming terrible day:

I looked, and behold, there was a great earthquake, and the sun became black as sackcloth, the full moon became like blood, and the stars in the sky fell to the earth as the fig tree sheds its winter fruit when shaken by a gale. **— Revelation 6:12–13 (ESV)**

God has filled the earth with enough of His grace that it has held the fullness of evil back; one day, however, God will remove common grace, and the destruction will be bitter and worldwide. The prophet Joel spoke of this terrible day centuries before John was even born. Joel wrote:

The earth quakes before them; the heavens tremble. The sun and the moon are darkened, and the stars withdraw their shining. The LORD utters his voice his army, for his camp is exceedingly great; he who executes his word is powerful. For the day of the LORD is great and very awesome; who can endure it? **— Joel 2:10–11 (ESV)**

On this great and terrible day of God's wrath, people will reap and sow according to their actions. It is easy to fall into the pit of declaring that God isn't aware of circumstances here on earth when on the contrary, He has allowed them for His glory, and personally comforts His people.

WORKBOOK

Chapter Eleven Questions

Question: How can you, in your personal life, head into darkness to find the light?

_____

_____

_____

_____

_____

_____

_____

_____

_____

_____

Question: How is the red horse present in today's society?

_____

_____

_____

_____

_____

_____

_____

_____

_____

_____

Question: Describe a time in your life when God allowed a painful circumstance, but you still knew He was sovereign over it?

_____

_____

_____

_____

_____

_____

_____

_____

_____

_____

_____

_____

Action: When Jesus returns, every wrong will be avenged, and humanity will reap what it has sown. God's people will no longer wait for His promises for they will be completely fulfilled. Now is the time to sow in preparation for the day of His return.

Chapter Eleven Notes

CHAPTER TWELVE

The Seal of Grace

*Jesus said to them: "I am the bread of life. Whoever comes to me shall not hunger and whoever believes in me shall never thirst. But I said to you that have seen me and yet do not believe. All that the Father gives me will come to me, and whoever comes to me I will never cast out. For I have come down from heaven, not to do my own will but the will of him who sent me. And this is the will of him who sent me, that I should lose nothing of all that he has given me, but raise it up on the last day. For this is the will of my Father, that everyone who looks on the Son and believes in him should have eternal life, and I will raise him up on the last day." — **John 6:35–40 (ESV)***

*After this I saw four angels standing at the four corners of the earth, holding back the four winds of the earth, that no wind might blow on earth or sea or against any tree. — **Revelation 7:1 (ESV)***

Both John 6:35–40 and Revelation 7:1 were written within the context of the common grace of God holding back the fullness of evil's effects. As bad as things may appear on earth, God is actually holding back wrath and judgment on humanity.

A different type of seal was referenced next:

> *Then I saw another angel ascending from the rising of the sun, with the seal of the living God, and he called with a loud voice to the four angels who had been given power to harm earth and sea, saying, "Do not harm the earth or the sea or the trees, until we have sealed the servants of our God on their foreheads."—* **Revelation 7:2–3 (ESV)**

John began to describe a different seal, one the voice from heaven said provided protection for God's people. It was not a number, and not a mark but rather a covering.

The moment you said yes to Jesus Christ, you were justified, forgiven, and sealed in the Holy Spirit. Paul's letter to the Ephesians teaches the Holy Spirit represents a down payment, or a deposit guaranteeing something better is ahead for those who trust Jesus (Ephesians 1:14). Thus, the Spirit is a covering. This covering does not remove believers from hardship but carries them through suffering.

So these "unsealings" are more than compensated for by God's seal. The seal of the Holy Spirit is a picture of the Exodus. Each family was instructed to mark the lintel and the mantle of their door with the blood of a perfect, unblemished lamb. This blood would cover or seal the firstborn son of the family protecting him as the death angel passed over their marked home.

God's deliverance is always at work. The same way the firstborn son was sealed in Exodus is the way every believer in Christ is sealed today. He is calling churches to know this and trust Him. He knew people in the first century were feeling pressure, and He knows people today are too; He was assuring both they were and are securely in His grip.

Jesus put it this way: "In the world you will have tribulation. But take heart; I have overcome the world" (John 16:33 ESV). He didn't say that on this earth you will have trouble and He will evacuate you from it. Rather, He said He will be with you in your troubles.

All people will experience *thlipsis* at some point in their life, whether it be a pink slip at work, a spouse who leaves unexpectedly, an accident, or an illness. There *will* be trouble on earth. Some brothers and sisters in Christ live in places of the world where gathering together to worship God could mean death—tribulation beyond what can be fathomed!

Looking outside the borders of twenty-first century America, it's much easier to see tribulation is very real and a result of sin—and no one is exempt. Why would God allow this?

This is where faith becomes real.

Christianity is not about a nice sermon once a week without a change in behavior and attitude. No, it is living out what one believes at all times and in every facet of life. It is continually clinging to God's presence not because He gives good things but simply because He is God. Sometimes this is hard to embrace.

The Multitude

And I heard the number of the sealed, 144,000, sealed from every tribe of the sons of Israel. —
Revelation 7:4 (ESV)

Who are the 144,000? Revelation 7:5–8 continues to list 12,000 from the tribe of Judah, 12,000 from the tribe of Reuben, and 12,000 each from Gad, Asher, Naphtali, Manasseh, Simeon, Levi, Issachar, Zebulun, Joseph, and Benjamin.

After this I looked, and behold, a great multitude that no one could number, from every nation, from all tribes and peoples and languages, standing before the throne and before the Lamb, clothed in white robes, with palm branches in their hands, and crying out with a loud voice, "Salvation belongs to our God who sits on the throne, and to the Lamb!" —
Revelation 7:9–10 (ESV)

John saw all the followers and believers of God from the beginning of time to the end—so many he couldn't number them. He *heard* a number, 144,000, but he *saw* a countless multitude.

Every nation, every tribe, every people group, and every language—all were standing. That is the picture God described in Genesis 11. Believers will experience each other, this earth, and their communities in a beautiful way. There will be no division, no annihilation through conquest, no poverty, and no death.

You will be standing, too.

Standing by the Throne

> *And all of the angels were standing around the throne and around the elders and the four living creatures, and they fell on their faces before the throne and worshiped God, saying, "Amen! Blessings and glory and wisdom and thanksgiving and honor and power and might be to our God forever and ever! Amen." —* **Revelation 7:11–12 (ESV)**

Those who are faithful will stand by God as the angels do, no matter how difficult life becomes, through increased tribulation and dark days—no matter that trials and battles escalate beyond imagination. The faithful ones belong to the One who created all things and who is sovereign over all things.

Consider two things Jesus has done for you that should change the way you go about each day of your life. His blood covers one thing in your life, but the cross covers another.

The blood of the lamb forgives you of your sins. Theologically, the word is called *justification*. You are *justified* by the atoning work or the sacrifice of Jesus on the cross. When God looks at you, you look just as if you have never sinned. Your sins past, present, and future are dealt with.

The cross deals more with overcoming the nature within that wants to keep sinning. Blood covers your sins, and you are forgiven, but the cross deals with the core issue of brokenness. Paul wrote about this to the Galatian church: "I have been crucified with Christ. It is no longer I who live, but Christ who lives in me" (Galatians 2:20 ESV).

He also taught in Romans 8 how Jesus' blood covers the sins in your life but how the cross helps you put that sinful nature to death. One of the reasons so many followers of the Rabbi Jesus remain stuck in their life is because while they have accepted the blood of Christ, they have not appropriated the cross of Christ.

Apart from the cross, people still receive forgiveness, but they do not experience the transformation that takes place upon allowing Jesus into the deepest parts of their heart and soul. This is where followers of Jesus admit and acknowledge hurts, habits, and hang-ups, and release them to Jesus.

When you said yes to Jesus, you were covered completely. God will carry you through. However, do you want more than a safety net? Do you want the divine life? Do you long for the higher life—His life—to be infused in you in such a way that you begin to see change and transformation?

There is a remedy. The remedy comes with Jesus' blood and the cross. That is why God's people were wearing white robes—a picture of purity. Palm branches stand for victory. Those made righteous by the blood of the Lamb are victorious. They were victors. They may not have lived perfect lives, but in the end, they stood.

The book of Ephesians discusses the importance of putting on the armor of God, not to defeat the enemy per say, but so that when the "day of evil comes, you may be able to stand your ground, and after everything, to stand" (Ephesians 6:13). If you have said yes to Jesus in your life, you are one of those who stands. Jesus' blood ensures this.

> Then one of the elders addressed me, saying, "Who are these, clothed in white robes, and from where have they come? I said to him, 'Sir, you know.' And he said to me, These are the ones coming out of the great tribulation. They have washed their robes. Therefore they are before the throne of God, and serve him day and night in his temple; and he who sits on the throne will shelter them with his presence. — **Revelation 7:13–15 (ESV)**

The relevant concept here is *shekinah*, which indicates protection—again, not the removal of suffering but the protection of God to carry you through. From the word *shakam* in the Old Testament, we get the phrase *shekinah* glory—the glory that appeared to signify God's divine presence as a pillar of cloud by day and fire by night. This presence let the Israelites know God was with them as they traveled through the wilderness. They were protected.

Jesus not only justifies, but He also protects.

Revelation 7:13–15 is a snapshot in the midst of a brief interlude between the sixth and seventh seal where John is privileged to see a snippet of heaven—and it's the only picture available to believers today. It includes terms about the millennial kingdom the prophets Isaiah and Ezekiel also used.

The heartbeat of this passage is that the Lamb, in the midst of the throne, will be the tribulation saints' shepherd and He will guide them to springs of living water (Revelation 7:16). There He will "shelter them with his presence" (Revelation 7:15 ESV).

John wrapped up Revelation 7 with Jesus' tender assurance for those who love Him: one day, God will wipe away every tear from their eyes (v. 17). There is a time coming, unknown to any man, where God will right every wrong.

What a role reversal!

The psalmist wrote of this day in Psalm 23, echoing language John used in Revelation:

> *The Lord is my shepherd; I shall not want. He makes me lie down in green pastures. He leads me beside still waters. He restores my soul.* **—Psalm 23:1–3 (ESV)**

This is what Jesus, Shepherd of souls, does in tribulation; He leads and restores. Though external pressure may press in, there is a shepherd who is watching over you all the time.

WORKBOOK

Chapter Twelve Questions

Question: Can you feel the seal of God on your soul? How do you know He has covered you?

_____

_____

_____

_____

_____

_____

_____

_____

_____

_____

Question: Have you accepted the blood of Jesus and the cross? How has your life changed because of those gifts?

_____

_____

_____

_____

_____

_____

_____

_____

_____

_____

_____

Question: How is Jesus shepherding you and your life?

_____

_____

_____

_____

_____

_____

_____

_____

_____

_____

_____

_____

Action: Jesus is the Good Shepherd who will protect His sheep in every circumstance. It is time to begin living as though you are protected by His presence and to respond in gratitude with worship. It is what you were designed to do.

Chapter Twelve Notes

CHAPTER THIRTEEN

Of Silence and Trumpets

When the Lamb opened the seventh seal, there was silence in heaven for about a half hour. **— Revelation 8:1 (ESV)**

Have you ever had that friend who really listened to you? Perhaps that friend was talking, and suddenly you said something that caused you both to lock eyes; you know you're being heard, and you feel safe and valued. You feel *known*.

The world is full of noise and competing sounds, full of people constantly talking but never listening. When the Lamb opened the seventh seal, there was absolute deafening silence in heaven. How incredible God is! Worship filled the throne room of God nonstop, but for thirty minutes there was silence in heaven. Imagine angels saying nothing; no shouts, no trumpets or harps sounding—all the heavenly noise that fills the throne room of heaven—dissipates. Then, in the silence, God listens to every prayer that has ever been prayed.

God wants His people to know He hears them. He is the God who listens, and He responds to prayer. This truth should bring great hope!

Revelation 8:1 reveals what is known as the seven trumpets, the judgment of the seventh seal. Before jumping into what happened with the first trumpet, consider for a moment why John may have received this revelation.

Genesis-Powered Prayer

Prayer—the most powerful spiritual weapon believers have in their arsenal—is often forgotten, locked away in obscurity, available but misunderstood. Prayer rightly understood and practiced is a gift God gives reminding His children He has a shared causality. Prayer is not a weak plea. It is infused with Genesis power.

John received this revelation, I believe, because he was a man steeped in prayer; he listened to God, and God listened—and revealed to John a glimpse of the mystery of what is to come.

John was the last living disciple, and Rome did not want to contend with him anymore. He was still a threat even though he was quite old. Exiled on the Greek island of Patmos, John likely spent his days in prayer and was in Spirit on the Lord's Day (Revelation 1:10). He was completely enraptured and caught up in all the energy that created the universe, unified in mind and spirit with the Father, Son, and Holy Spirit. As a result, in the midst of unimaginable exile and hardship, he received the *apocalypses*: the revelation of Jesus Christ.

Why the Shofar?

Then I saw the seven angels who stand before God, and seven trumpets were given to them. — ***Revelation 8:2 (ESV)***

The seven angels are most commonly known as the angels of the presence. Jewish tradition holds these seven angels stand in God's presence.[100] We read about them in some of the apocryphal books like Tobit, which tells us there are seven angels who attend God (Tobit 12:15). Traditionally, they are called by names like Raphael, Gabriel, and Michael—the suffix *el* being a word for God, which is only appropriate since they are said to be closest to God. Always ready to move on His behalf, they stand ready with their trumpets. Readers may immediately think of silver trumpets, but the initial image that springs to mind is likely incorrect: these trumpets are actually shofars.[101]

The shofar, a biblical instrument, was a ram's horn. This was the biblical version of the trumpet. Just imagine trumpets were used to play different themes for different purposes throughout the Bible.

Accompanying Armies in Battle

God's instrument to lead Israel into the Promised Land, Joshua, had a magnificent encounter with the commander of the armies of the Lord. This is known in Christian theology as a "Christophany." A Christophany is an appearance of Jesus Christ in the Old Testament. The Lord told Joshua:

> *See, I have given Jericho into your hand, with its king and mighty men of valor. You shall march around the city, all the men of war going around the city once. Thus shall you do for six days. Seven priests shall bear seven trumpets of rams' horns before the ark. On the seventh day you shall march around the city seven times, and the priests shall blow the trumpets. And when they make a long blast with the ram's horn, when you hear the sound of the trumpet, then all the people shall shout with a great shout, and the wall of the city will fall down flat.* **— Joshua 6:2–5 (ESV)**

The Lord commanded Israel's armies to march around Jericho six times in silence. But on the seventh day, they were to march seven times, blowing trumpets—a "long blast with the ram's horn" (Joshua 6:5 ESV).

Revelation 8 echoes this scene in Joshua 6. A period of silence was followed by the clamor of the shofar—to usher in a triumphant demonstration of the Lord's might.

Calling the Congregation to Assembly

Numbers 10 reveals another purpose for using trumpets in Scripture. In this chapter, the Lord commanded Moses to craft two silver trumpets. Moses gave them to the Levites for a couple of purposes, including to call the congregation to assembly. When the trumpet sound blasted, all of Israel was supposed to gather; it meant God had a message for His people.

Beginning Festivals

Certain religious festivals, including Yom Kippur (the Day of Atonement) and Yom Teruah (Day of Trumpet Blasts, or the Feast of Trumpets), were begun with a trumpet blast. The ram's horn would be blown again as sacrifices were made on Yom Kippur.

Proclaiming the Year of Jubilee

Trumpets were also to be blown on the year of Jubilee:

> *Count off seven sabbath years—seven times seven years—so that the seven sabbath years amount to a period of forty-nine years. Then have the trumpet sounded everywhere on the tenth day of the seventh month; on the Day of Atonement sound the trumpet throughout your land.* **— Leviticus 25:8–9 (NIV)**

Every fifty years God designed Israel to celebrate a Jubilee year. From the forty-ninth to the fiftieth year, all debts were forgiven. Slaves were freed. Property sold to another because of financial hardship was reverted to the original owner (Leviticus 25:9–13). It was an equalizing year—a year of freedom and forgiveness.

Interestingly, Jesus began His ministry during a Jubilee year—proclaiming the beginning of this year of freedom and forgiveness by reading from the scroll of Isaiah.

The Rapturing Up

When Jesus returns, there will be a blast of a shofar that will announce to the world that the King of Kings is returning to rule and reign from Jerusalem. Paul described this in 1 Thessalonians 4:16 when he said, "For the Lord himself will descend from heaven with a cry of command, with the voice of an archangel, and with the sound of the trumpet of God. And the dead in Christ will rise first" (ESV).

These are known as the *trumpets of thirds*. Damage begins, but only in thirds. These trumpet blasts mean the end is not yet. These trumpets serve as warnings; those who believe in Jesus are protected, but those who are not in the Lamb will not be covered from the plagues—in the same way, the Egyptians were not protected from the ten plagues in the book of Exodus.

Prayers in a Bowl of Incense

> *Another angel came and stood at the altar with a golden censer, and he was given much incense to offer with the prayers of all of the saints on the golden altar before the throne, and the smoke of the incense with the prayers of the saints rose before God from the hand of the angel. Then the angel took the censer and filled it with fire from the altar and threw it on the earth, and there were peals of thunder, rumblings, flashes of lightning, and an earthquake. —* **Revelation 8:3–5 (ESV)**

John described an altar of incense before entering the Holy of Holies. The smoke of the incense "with the prayers of all of the saints" rose before God from the hand of the angel (Revelation 8:4 ESV). In the midst of silence, God heard every prayer. Then the heavenly fire was placed in this bowl of incense, and God's people's prayers were returned.

What a tremendous source of encouragement to know that God not only hears prayers, but they are *physically* before Him. He sees them, he hears them, and they haven't been overlooked, misplaced, or swept under the rug. Even though you haven't received the answer you're looking for, He holds your prayer and appropriates exactly what needs to be done with it. The incense is a picture of purifying the prayers that people pray before God.

Have you ever prayed in a non-holy way? Paul wrote the Holy Spirit's job is to intercede with God's people with groanings "too deep for words" (Romans 8:26); the Holy Spirit helps believers pray. When Christians lift up their imperfect prayers to God, He adds His incense to them and purifies what they pray with fire. He removes the egoism or the darkness out of them and empowers them with His Holy Spirit. What happens with those prayers? They are hurled back into the earth as an answer.

Many people grow angry at God when they read this. Most people want to see justice done. Most people want to see poverty eliminated and violence ended. But God does something with His people's prayers even if it's not the response they anticipate.

Prayer isn't something a person *ought* to do or something only a Christian does. Prayer isn't giving a shopping list to God. Prayer, rightfully understood, is an act of causality working with the Divine to change things on earth.

When you have prayed, and it seems there is no answer, there are a few options to consider. Sometimes you may not be ready to receive from God what He has for you. Your foundation may not yet be strong enough for what you are asking for. God knows when His people ask for things that might destroy them, so He allows things to happen in life to strengthen them and build a foundation so He can bless them with what *He* longs for.

Sometimes the things Christians pray for are full of selfish gain; God may not answer a person because He may be purifying the prayers. And sometimes it's just not time yet. But remember, God is always up to something.

When you pray for someone, expect something to happen in God's time.

Never think prayer is just a last, desperate attempt to cause something to happen. It is divine power. God moves when you pray. Oh, the greatest gift followers of Jesus have is the power inherent in prayer. Prayers enter God's presence where they are purified and empowered; they then reenter earth with divine force. Things do change according to the sovereign plan of God.

The Trumpet Plagues and Wormwood

Next, the third of the seven trumpet judgments of the seventh seal occurs:

Now the seven angels who had the seven trumpets prepared to blow them.

*The first angel blew his trumpet, and there followed hail and fire, mixed with blood, and these were thrown upon the earth. And a third of the earth was burned up, and a third of the trees were burnt up, and all green grass was burnt up. — **Revelation 8:6–7 (ESV)***

The trumpet plagues John described next aren't listed in the same chronological order as the Exodus plagues, but there are obvious similarities. In Revelation 8:6–7, John saw the earth pounded with fire and hail mixed with blood.

When this happens, there will be no safe place to run. Human beings won't be able to run to the sky; there will be no safe place on the earth, and there will be no safe place on the sea. The only safe place will be with God, under His covering.

John next described what happened when the second angel sounded his horn:

The second angel blew his trumpet, and something like a great mountain, burning with fire, was thrown into the sea, and a third of the sea became blood. A third of the living creatures in the sea died, and a third of the ships were destroyed.

*The third angel blew his trumpet and a great star fell from heaven blazing like a torch and it fell on a third of the rivers and on the springs of water. The name of the star is wormwood, a third of the waters became wormwood, and many people died from the water, because it had been made bitter. — **Revelation 8:8–11 (ESV)***

This third trumpet upsets the earth's lakes and rivers, turning them from fresh water to bitter water, perhaps making it impossible to drink. In fact, the name "wormwood" comes from the Greek word, *apsinthion,* and means bitter.[102]

Whatever was supposed to bring refreshment—which was Israel's job, to bring the Torah and spiritual nourishment to the world—will become bitter.

Key imagery reflected in Revelation 8:8–11 echoes Exodus 15. The entire nation of Israel had left Egypt, and the Egyptian army had been engulfed in the Red Sea; miraculously, Israel made it to dry land on the other side. In resulting joy, Moses sang an incredible song—his victory song, the song of Moses—and Israel continued on with its journey. But the people ran out of water quickly, and they arrived at Marah. At Marah, the water was undrinkable because it was bitter. Moses, at the Lord's command, threw a log into the water, and it became sweet (Exodus 15:25). Though they had just been delivered, the sea had just closed up, and God had provided refreshing water, it wasn't good enough. The people grumbled, and the entire nation said, "Why, now, have you brought us up from Egypt, to kill us and our children and our livestock with thirst?" (Exodus 17:3 NASB).

Recall in Exodus 15:25 the tree God instructed to be thrown in the water. When this tree touched the bitter water, it became sweet and refreshing. The Scriptures foretell the Messiah would one day be executed on a tree. This is profound imagery of the only thing that can turn wormwood—bitter water—sweet: Jesus, whom Israel had rejected.

Until a person accepts Jesus in their life, all the wormwood experiences make their "water" bitter; there is no escape from that. There is no way to receive this living water apart from Jesus; without Him, the water will always be bitter.

Repent, realign, pray, and draw near to Messiah Jesus, who offers living water that will satisfy every thirst. Cling to His promise, that the water He gives "will become ... a spring of water welling up to eternal life" (John 4:14 ESV).

WORKBOOK

Chapter Thirteen Questions

Question: What is a shofar? What were the various ways it is used in the Bible?

_____

_____

_____

_____

_____

_____

_____

_____

_____

_____

_____

Question: Why do you think your prayers are not always answered in the way you expect? Give an example from your life.

_____

_____

_____

_____

_____

_____

_____

_____

_____

_____

Question: When have you encountered "wormwood" in your life? What is this best way to respond to wormwood experiences?

_____

_____

_____

_____

_____

_____

_____

_____

_____

_____

_____

_____

Action: Your prayers enter God's presence, are purified, are empowered, and reenter the earth with divine force. Seek God and His covering—the only safe place.

Chapter Thirteen Notes

_____

_____

_____

_____

_____

_____

_____

_____

_____

_____

_____

_____

_____

_____

_____

_____

_____

_____

_____

_____

_____

_____

CHAPTER FOURTEEN

Demon's Demise

At the end of Revelation 8, John said:

*Then I looked, and I heard an eagle crying with a loud voice as it flew directly overhead, "Woe, woe, woe to those who dwell on the earth, at the blasts of the other trumpets that the three angels are about to blow." —**Revelation 8:13 (ESV)***

The first four trumpets bring about a massive tribulation, causing the destruction of Jerusalem in AD 70. Jesus had warned the city's inhabitants about this in Matthew 24:

Jesus left the temple and was going away, when his disciples came to point out to him the buildings of the temple. But he answered them, "You see all these, do you not? Truly, I say to you, there will not be left here one stone upon another that will not be thrown down."
*— **Matthew 24:1–2 (ESV)***

The book of Revelation, as seen so far, focuses largely on the *spiritual* battle happening behind the scenes of the physical battle. Satan has already lost, but until Jesus returns, the spiritual battle will continue. When the church forgets this truth, it loses valuable ground.

The prophet Zechariah quoted Jesus in Luke 1 saying: "Because of the tender mercy of our God, whereby the sunrise shall visit us from on high to give light to those who sit in darkness and in the shadow of death, to guide our feet into the way of peace" (Luke 1:78–79 ESV). Christians are still living in the aftershock of the ills spelled out in Revelation; conquest, violence, poverty, and death.

The enemy might think he is winning because of mounting destruction, violence, and poverty, but love will win. God has Satan on a short leash; He has a plan in place. He is sovereign and controls all things, and He is allowing this evil to erupt so that He can finally put it down and His people can experience the life He created them to experience. That day is coming.

Moving into Chapter 9—The Abyss

Up to this point, John has described a heavenly, spiritual battle. Now, John shifts his focus to a physical battle on earth.

And the fifth angel blew his trumpet, and I saw a star fallen from heaven to earth, and he was given the key to the shaft of the bottomless pit. He opened the shaft

> *of the bottomless pit, and from the shaft rose smoke*
> *like the smoke of a great furnace, and the sun and the*
> *air were darkened with the smoke from the shaft.*
> *Then from the smoke came locusts on the earth, and*
> *they were given power like the power of scorpions of*
> *the earth. They were told not to harm the grass of the*
> *earth or any green plant or any tree, but only those*
> *people who do not have the seal of God on their*
> *foreheads.* **—Revelation 9:1–4 (ESV)**

John described a star that has fallen from heaven to earth, who is given the key to what is described as a "bottomless pit." The Greek word for "bottomless pit" is *abyssos*, which means, "bottomless, pit, unbounded, or immeasurable death."[103] This is why some Bible translations use the word abyss for this bottomless pit.

The abyss isn't hell; it's not the ultimate end, which is the lake of fire that John speaks of toward the end of the book. The abyss is the intermediary place where God has thrown the fallen angels and demons He has bound. John describes hell unleashed on earth. This angel with the key has been given the authority to do that, pointing to the permissive will of God.

In the gospel of Luke, the disciple describes Jesus' encounter with a man who was demonically possessed. Jesus comes before him, and the demons terrorizing this man begin to shout: "What have you to do with me, Jesus, Son of the Most High God? I beg you, do not torment me." (Luke 4:34 ESV). Jesus asked the demon his name, and the demon responded "Legion," for many demons had entered the man (Luke 8:30). Then, the demons begged Jesus not to command them to depart in into the abyss (Luke 8:31). Demons know Jesus has authority and power to bind them and send them into the abyss.

Fallen Angels and Demons

There's a difference between a fallen angel and a demon—they are not the same thing. Angels have physicality, which means they can materialize. Demons are formless spirits, always looking for something physical to attach themselves to, and they long to be worshipped.[104]

In Luke 10:17–20, Jesus sent seventy-two of His followers out to do ministry. When they returned, they were to report to Jesus everything that had happened. Scripture says they "returned with joy and said, 'Lord, even the demons are subject to us in your name!' And he said to them, 'I saw Satan fall like lightning from heaven'" (ESV).

Luke 10 clearly references the star that falls to earth from heaven in Revelation 9. The star that has fallen is called *him,* which indicates it is a person and not a thing.

This fallen star is none other than Satan. It is Satan who is given the key to unleash violent and terrible things on Jerusalem—but not those with "the seal of God on their foreheads" (Revelation 9:4 ESV).

He next portrayed Satan bringing forth locusts with scorpion-like stingers to torment those without God's seal.

In appearance the locusts were like horses prepared for battle: on their heads were what looked like crowns of gold; their faces were like human faces, their hair like women's hair, and their teeth like lions' teeth; they had breastplates like breastplates of iron, and the noise of their wings was like the noise of many chariots with horses rushing into battle. — **Revelation 9:7–9 (ESV)**

The noise was probably like the noise of a stadium during a concert or football game. And this roaring swarm of locusts, according to John, was able to sting like scorpions, with tails that hold the power to hurt people for five months (Revelation 9:10).

Attempting to extrapolate this passage of John's letter from AD 70 into the future misses the whole point of what John is trying to communicate. These images of the locusts were describing a particular group of people who were Rome's greatest threat on the east side of the Euphrates River,—the Parthians. The Parthians were known for their incredible marksmanship—they were able to shoot arrows backward across the tail of their horse.[105]

In this scene, God allows evil to destroy evil strategically. Remember, this battle is occurring primarily in the spiritual dimension, not the physical dimension. Thus, spiritual powers move the physical powers—like Rome and Parthia—to destroy each other, while the Christians escape.

Authority in Christ

Behold, I have given you authority to tread on serpents and scorpions, and over all the power of the enemy, and nothing shall hurt you. — **Luke 10:19 (ESV)**

Luke reminded his readers that they have been given all authority over the enemy. Believers should rejoice that they have power over supernatural forces of darkness! In 1 John 4:4, the apostle affirmed this saying, "He who is in you is greater than he who is in the world" (ESV). A Christian never has to fear the demonic.

A British evangelist who ministered at the turn of the century named Smith Wigglesworth had a unique way of responding to demonic activities. One night Wigglesworth was in bed and sensed an evil presence in his room. (I know people who have this same gift of discernment—being highly sensitive to the demonic). Sensing the demon, he looked at it and saw a sort of black fog at the foot of his bed. Smith responded to this manifestation by saying, "Oh, it's only you." Then he went back to sleep.[106]

That's the authority you have as a follower and a believer in Jesus Christ. Most Christians have no idea the extent of the authority granted them by Jesus. The authority God gave Jesus is the same authority you have. You need not fear anything in the demonic realm. Demons can mess with you, and they can toy with you, but they can never overcome you. They can't possess you.

The believer's job is to be faithful, a peacemaker, and a blessing. They are not to respond to violence with violence. There is no place in the Christian's life for that. God will handle retribution and justice for He says, "Vengeance is mine" (Deuteronomy 32:35 ESV).

Repentance and Alignment

God allows evil to attack evil so that people will arrive at a point where they acknowledge their need for Him. God's desire is repentance. The looming question for Christians, then, is: *How low does the bottom have to sink before people turn to God?*

Repentance means we confess, "Okay God, I realize and agree with you that I have been doing some things that aren't in alignment with how You want me to live." Repentance is agreeing with God and then walking in God's direction, which I call "repentance and alignment." Therefore, repentance is not a scary or nasty word; it is a life-giving word that appears throughout the pages of the Bible. God longs for those He created to turn their heart over to Him so that He might save them from the conquest, violence, poverty, and death that hold sway in the world and are described in Revelation.

Even in the midst of crazy locust demonic invasions, the seven churches John discussed in Revelation 1–3 are preserved. God is watching over them, and they realize their need for repentance.

I, too, long for every single person who hasn't yet encountered Jesus to meet Him—I want them to experience His beauty and grace, rather than His wrath.

The only way to ensure this is by being a blessing—by showing people the tangible touch of God and what God has in store for them.

Pray for healing, restoration, and for people's eyes to be opened to the truth of who Jesus is. Don't hammer them with bullhorns and picket signs, but rather overwhelm them with love and compassion. Jesus taught what was most important: "By this all people will know that you are my disciples, if you have love for one another" (John 13:35 ESV).

The calling card of belonging to God is showing His love.

WORKBOOK

Chapter Fourteen Questions

Question: What is your reaction to the concept of having the same authority as Jesus? What are the implications of this authority for your life?

_____

_____

_____

_____

_____

_____

_____

_____

_____

_____

_____

_____

Question: Why should Christians not respond to violence with violence?

_____

_____

_____

_____

_____

_____

_____

_____

_____

_____

Question: How can you overwhelm non-believers with love and compassion?

_____

_____

_____

_____

_____

_____

_____

_____

_____

_____

_____

Question: How would you define repentance? What is one thing you need to repent of today?

_____

_____

_____

_____

_____

_____

_____

_____

_____

_____

_____

Action: God allows evil to strategically destroy evil while His people escape. All He asks is that you repent and turn toward Him. Then, the same authority Jesus possessed is the authority that you have!

Chapter Fourteen Notes

_____

_____

_____

_____

_____

_____

_____

_____

_____

_____

_____

_____

_____

_____

_____

_____

_____

_____

_____

CHAPTER FIFTEEN

Living in Mystery

Human beings have this insatiable desire to know about things that haven't yet taken place. They want to know all things from the past but also what is going to happen in the future. Often, people approach the book of Revelation assuming they will obtain answers to the future: What is going to happen? What's the future going to look like?

Yet living in mystery is not only okay, but it is actually healthy. It is not necessary to know everything about everything. Living in mystery allows God's people to keep thinking, dreaming, and wondering what is out there and what's happening. What is it going to be like tomorrow, next week, a year from now, or ten years from now? This uncertainty spurs God's people on toward hope. Mystery is absolutely okay. Remember Einstein's observation that anyone unfamiliar with mystery "is as good as dead. His eyes are closed."[107]

Living in mystery is a beautiful thing.

Big Angel, Little Scroll

As John's vision continued, His focus came back down to earth:

> *Then I saw another mighty angel coming down from heaven, wrapped in a cloud, with a rainbow over his head, and his face was like the sun, and his legs like pillars of fire.* **— Revelation 10:1 (ESV)**

The images of heaven of someone wrapped in a cloud with a rainbow overhead would normally point to Christ. However, in John's vision, this picture is *not* of Jesus; the Scripture states it is another "mighty angel." Remember Jesus was never an angel; rather, He has always been fully God and fully man.

However, this angel represents Messiah Jesus 100 percent. John sees a reflection of who Jesus is in everything. This angel brings the words of the Messiah, and Revelation 10:1 says the angel's face "was like the sun," shining just as Moses' did when he came down from the mountain after meeting God. Clearly, this angel both saw God and was also a representative of Jesus and His Word.

Then, John saw the angel open a scroll:

> *He had a little scroll open in his hand. And he set his right foot on the sea, and his left foot on the land, and called out with a loud voice, like a lion roaring. When he called out, the seven thunders sounded.* **— Revelation 10:2–3 (ESV)**

Recall in Revelation 5 the scroll Jesus held. The Greek word for "scroll" in Revelation 5 is different from the type of scroll John spoke about in Revelation 10. The Greek word in Revelation 5 is *biblion*,[108] but in Revelation 10 the word is *biblaridion*—"little scroll."[109]

Notice the angel's right foot is on the sea while his left foot is on land. This symbolic act reveals authority has been given to the angel—authority over all of creation to deliver this message boldly.

It is a loud message. Don't miss God's message for you; Psalm 29:3 says, "The voice of the Lord is over the waters. The God of glory thunders, the Lord, over many waters" (ESV). Job 37:5 says, "God thunders wondrously with his voice; he does great [and mysterious] things that we cannot comprehend" (ESV).

Secrets in Thunder

*And when the seven thunders had sounded, I was about to write, but I heard a voice from heaven saying, "Seal up what the seven thunders have said, and do not write it down." — **Revelation 10:4 (ESV)***

John no sooner received this message when he was immediately told not to write it down. The mystery remains; God's people do not need to know everything He is going to do.

God does command believers to, "Keep this Book of the Law always on your lips; meditate on it day and night" (Joshua 1:8 NIV). Those who are students of the Scriptures may love digging into the Greek and Hebrew meanings of words to help guide them deeper in their studies. Though studying the Bible may help people understand the Word better, there will always remain a thread of mystery; God will not answer every question this side of heaven.

Every person alive lives in mystery—they live in mystery of their past and their present. They also live in mystery of the future—and this applies in two ways.

First, it applies to the spiritual world. No person understands what God is doing all the time, or perfectly discerns the meanings behind every verse of Scripture.

Second, it also applies to someone's personal life. People may never receive answers for why negative things happened in their life, though they may spend a lifetime trying.

God's message is a mystery. When I read that last verse in Revelation, part of me asks, "Why did God allow John to see that, anyway? Did the vision help John? Why was it okay for him to see something but not write about it? Why did certain things help the passage, the seven churches that received the letters and the vision? Why did that help them if they weren't going to know what took place?" I wonder all these things, and I think the answer is simple: God's message is a mystery, and it's okay.

But believers still have the hope of knowledge for the future. One day, all God's mysteries will be uncovered and fulfilled—and everything will make sense. Imagine the day when every question will be answered:

And the angel whom I saw standing on the sea and on the land raised his right hand to heaven and swore by him who lives forever and ever, who created heaven and what is in it, the earth and what is in it, and the sea and what is in it, that there would be no more delay, but that in the days of the trumpet call to be sounded by the seventh angel, the mystery of God would be fulfilled, just as he announced to his servants the prophets. — **Revelation 10:5–7 (ESV)**

On this day, "the mystery of God [will] be fulfilled" (Revelation 10:7 ESV). What a glorious day this will be for those who trust Jesus!

John's Job

God gave John a specific assignment next:

Then the voice that I had heard from heaven spoke to me again, saying, "Go, take the scroll that is open in the hand of the angel who is standing on the sea and on the land." So I went to the angel and I told him to give me the little scroll. And he said to me, "Take and eat it; it will make your stomach bitter, but in your mouth it will be sweet as honey." And I took the little scroll from the hand of the angel and ate it. It was sweet as honey in my mouth, but when I had eaten it my stomach was made bitter. — **Revelation 10:8–10 (ESV)**

Picture this mighty angel, surrounded by a cloud, a brilliant rainbow encircling his head, legs like a pillar of fire, a face shining, and with one foot on the sand and on the sea. Imagine John approaching this mighty angel boldly, and demanding—not asking—"Give me the little scroll."

The angel told John to take the scroll and eat it—and out of obedience, he did so without question. The scroll was sweet as honey at first but bitter in his stomach.

What is this scroll, and why was it as sweet as honey? In Ezekiel 3, the prophet saw a similar vision. He too was commanded to eat a scroll described "as sweet as honey" (Ezekiel 3:3 ESV).

Though also described as sweet as honey, John's scroll became bitter, like wormwood. John's message was one of repentance. It was a message of woe, of lamentation, to redirect you away from what you are doing and move you closer to God.

And the Beat Goes On

Then, the angel gave John more specific instructions: "And I was told, 'You must again prophesy about many peoples and nations and languages and kings'" (Revelation 10:11 ESV). Though the scroll was bitter, John still had a job to do. John must continue to prophesy. Like John, even though is often difficult, believers need to continue to go out and share the message they have been given. God's message will continue.

Christians are called to continue sharing who Jesus is. Though there will be both successes and struggles, God's Word exhorts followers of Jesus to press on—especially within the body of believers. It is paramount Christians build each other up, encourage each other, and if necessary, share a message that for some will be bitter:

repent and believe, turn from wickedness, and believe Jesus is the Messiah.

Often, however, Christians are too scared to declare this message of who Jesus really is. They may be afraid of the judgment that might result, how they will look, or how it will be received. Nonetheless, believers must move forward in the example John gave with boldness, continuing in the knowledge it is okay to live in mystery.

You may not even know the reason for people's response. You may not know why you are judged simply for sharing the gospel. You may never understand these things until you are face to face with Jesus—and that's okay. Accept what Jesus has revealed to you and be bold with sharing that message. Be comforted by Paul's words: "My God will supply every need of yours according to his riches in glory in Christ Jesus" (Philippians 4:19 ESV).

Chapter Fifteen Questions

Question: What does it mean to you to live in mystery? How is this easy or difficult for you?

_____

_____

_____

_____

_____

_____

_____

_____

_____

_____

Question: How does it feel to know that one day all your questions will be answered?

_____

_____

_____

_____

_____

_____

_____

_____

_____

_____

_____

Question: What are some steps you can take to move away from negative influences in your life, and move closer to God?

_____

_____

_____

_____

_____

_____

_____

_____

_____

_____

_____

_____

Question: What is holding you back from sharing Jesus more? What steps can you take to change this?

_____

_____

_____

_____

_____

_____

_____

_____

_____

_____

_____

Action: You don't need to know everything about everything; living in mystery is a beautiful thing. God's message is a mystery. God's call on your life is to continue sharing who Jesus is—and this is enough.

Chapter Fifteen Notes

CHAPTER SIXTEEN

From a Different Angle

In a football game, cameramen often switch from one angle to another to catch details of a play that might reveal how close a player was to stepping on or off the line. From the first angle, you might not be able to see what another camera angle shows clearly.

That's what's happening in the book of Revelation: the way John described his vision is not unlike presenting multiple ESPN camera angles. The theological term for this phenomenon is *progressive parallelism.*[110] Revelation is not chronological storytelling. Every angle reveals a different nuance. John's narrative is presented in an overlaying, overlapping way—not chronologically.

Revelation 11 also introduces temple imagery. However, Revelation 11 is neither a discussion about a literal, ancient temple nor a future temple to be built on that site. Instead, John revealed a parable of the entire story of redemption—of which believers are a part of.

He was telling a story that primarily dealt with the death and resurrection of Jesus Christ and the empowerment of the church.

Measure by Measure

After John ate the scroll in Revelation 10, he "was given a measuring rod like a staff" (Revelation 11:1 ESV). Then he was told to:

> *Rise and measure the temple of God and the altar and those who worship there, but do not measure the court outside the temple; leave that out, for it is given over to the nations, and they will trample the holy city for forty-two months. — **Revelation 11:1–2 (ESV)***

The temple courts may have been trampled, but God has sealed, counted, and measured His bride, who is in His presence and worshiping in this picture of heaven. God is aware of my struggles, and He is involved when I suffer. Even when the rest of the world has gone south, God understands.

The Authority of the Supernatural

Two new characters are then introduced in Revelation 11:3, whom John calls "witnesses":

> *And I will grant authority to my two witnesses, and they will prophesy for 1,260 days, clothed in sackcloth. — **Revelation 11:3 (ESV)***

Three and one-half years—that is how long 1,260 days is. These witnesses in Revelation 11:3 will prophesy for more than three years; these two are "the two anointed ones" discussed in the book of Zechariah:

> Then I said to him, "What are these two olive trees on the left and the right of the lampstand?" And a second time I answered and said to him, "What are these two branches of the olive trees, which are beside the two golden pipes from which the golden oil is poured out?" He said to me, "Do you not know what these are?" I said, "No, my lord." Then he said, "These are the two anointed ones who stand by the Lord of the whole earth." — *Zechariah 4:11–14 (ESV)*

Jesus has given power and the authority to bring about signs and wonders to solidify the gospel presence. The church is still supposed to be the epicenter of the power and the movement of God intangible. It is this way in many parts of the world, but is not as evident in the West; here the church worships rationalism and science far more than the supernatural God of Scripture. He doesn't fit into the scope of logic and measurable science, which is one reason supernatural happenings do not occur in the West in this author's opinion. The normal Christian life is supposed to be a life surrounded and saturated with the power of God, and when it's not, something is missing.

Do you realize the same power that caused Christ to rise from the dead dwells in you? Do you believe it? Do you know it? When life becomes arduous, and trials engulf your strength, do you have confidence in the God of miracles, or do you just throw up a hopeful prayer? There is nothing God can't do. Under His sovereignty, when a believer says *God, move,* and they trust Him to move, it will happen. God has spoken to you, and He will not leave you alone. He has measured you, He has counted you, and He has sealed you.

Most importantly, God empowered you when He called you. Revelation 11 is a parable of God's ultimate story—the prophesying church talking about the good news, the power of God. God won't call you to speak to someone or to move somewhere without empowering you to actually do it. I have talked to many people who avoid responding to God's call by saying, "Well, I *think* God wants me to do this, but there is just no way I can." This is true; in your strength, you probably can't do much of anything for the kingdom.

When you feel God moving you to speak to a person you have been afraid to talk to, call on the Holy Spirit for assistance. Luke 12 avows, "the Holy Spirit will teach you in that very hour what you ought to say (Revelation 12:12 ESV). God has given you a spirit of power, not timidity (2 Timothy 1:7). He has imparted to you the authority of Jesus to move forward in victory.

What to Do When Evil Seems to Win

And when they [the two witnesses] have finished their testimony, the beast that arises from the bottomless pit will make war on them and conquer them and kill them, and their dead bodies will lie in the streets of the great city ... where their Lord was crucified." — **Revelation 11:7–8 (ESV)**

There are times when it seems that good is succumbing to evil—that evil is winning. Persecution of Christians worldwide is increasing in this day. There are many people who want to see the church suffer and ultimately defeated—but God has the church firmly in His hands.

The word for witness is the Greek word *martys* which means, in a legal sense, exactly how it is translated: "a witness."[111] John said these two who will testify to Christ would become martyrs. Their ministry will be short, and they will boldly preach the gospel—but they will die. However, Jesus will one day gather *all* those who belong to Him—including those who have been martyred—because He has measured His people.

Meanwhile, evil is on a short leash. God is sovereign, and His people are "cleaning up" until the second coming of Christ when God takes back what is rightfully His:

> Then the seventh angel blew his trumpet, and there were loud voices in heaven, saying, "The kingdom of the world has become the kingdom of our Lord and of his Christ, and he shall reign forever and ever." And the twenty-four elders who sit on their thrones before God fell on their faces and worshiped God, saying, "We give thanks to you, Lord God Almighty, who is and who was, for you have taken your great power and begun to reign." — **Revelation 11:16–17 (ESV)**

So, when it seems everything is falling apart in your personal life, and though it may appear the church has lost its effectiveness as a light to a lost world; remember,

God is always up to something. John made this clear as He described the beginning of the Lord's reign on earth.

The nations raged, but your wrath came, and the time for the dead to be judged, and for rewarding your servants, the prophets and saints, and those who fear your name, both small and great, and for destroying the destroyers of the earth.

Then God's temple in heaven was opened, and the ark of his covenant was seen within his temple. There was flashings of lightning, rumblings, peals of thunder, an earthquake, and heavy hail. — **Revelation 11:18–19 (ESV)**

Stand firm in the knowledge that God has a plan. Reclaim Holy Spirit theology that empowers the members of God's bride, the church, to be the living presence of God to others.

The church has given up its authority and sold its birthright, but it's time to take it back. It's time for the church to be the physical presence and representation of Jesus, which means stepping boldly out into the world with compassion, justice, beauty, truth, and grace— keeping God's mission in view so that even the worst of detractors will be undone by His love.

WORKBOOK

Chapter Sixteen Questions

Question: How have you, or those you know, experienced the power of God?

_____

_____

_____

_____

_____

_____

_____

_____

_____

_____

_____

_____

Question: What steps do you need to take to better internalize and live out the authority Jesus has already given you?

_____

_____

_____

_____

_____

_____

_____

_____

_____

Question: In what specific ways can you improve in terms of becoming the physical presence and representation of Christ to the world?

_____

_____

_____

_____

_____

_____

_____

_____

_____

_____

_____

_____

Action: Chapter 11 of the book of Revelation is a parable of God's ultimate story—the death and resurrection of Christ and empowerment of the church. It is time for the church—and for you—to be the physical presence and representation of Jesus.

Chapter Sixteen Notes

_____

_____

_____

_____

_____

_____

_____

_____

_____

_____

_____

_____

_____

_____

_____

_____

_____

_____

_____

_____

_____

_____

_____

CHAPTER SEVENTEEN

Understanding Symbols

The song of heaven has been sung; God gave John a glimpse of His ultimate victory to share with His people through the book of Revelation. In light of this, how should believers respond to a world that does not yet know it is lost?

Revelation 12 affords some key insights on how to react when the world lashes out against everything that is good, pure, and true. This is what the church needed to learn in John's day, and what it still needs to know today.

People tend to respond in kind, but Jesus didn't give His followers that option. Christians are called to a higher standard of ethics, a higher standard of living, and a higher standard of how they interact with people. They are even called to love those who hurt them, persecute them, and want them dead. Rather than retaliating, Jesus taught believers to respond with grace, mercy, and love. How is this possible in a world that believes the opposite? Even Jesus said, "You will be hated by everyone because of me" (Matthew 10:22 NIV).

It is only possible through prayer. Christians are to pray for their persecutors because revenge is not an option. God says vengeance is His alone (Romans 12:19).

The Mystery Woman of Revelation 12

After images of trumpet blasts, seals, and witnesses, John next described a troublesome scene.

> *A great sign appeared in heaven: a woman clothed with the sun, with the moon under her feet, and on her head a crown of twelve stars. She was pregnant and was crying out in birth pains and the agony of giving birth.—Revelation 12:1–2 (ESV)*

Many people read through Revelation 12 and come up with different ideas of who this woman giving birth might be. Some interpret the woman to be Mary, Jesus' mother, but a detailed read of the entirety of Revelation 12 indicates otherwise. Some believe the woman to be representative of the church; this is incorrect as well because the church does not birth the Messiah.

Corroborating this chapter with the rest of Scripture will reveal the prophets viewed righteous Israel, eschatological Israel, and the remnant of Israel as the mother of the future restored Israel. Thus, the woman represents Israel. As the prophet Micah wrote, speaking of this future restoration:

*And you, O tower of the flock, hill of the tower of Zion,
to you it shall come, the former dominion shall come,
kingship for the daughter of Jerusalem.* — ***Micah 4:8
(ESV)***

But why was the woman wearing a crown of twelve
stars? Genesis 37 provides a clue. Joseph, one of Jacob's
twelve sons, experienced a number of dreams. Genesis
37:9 says, "Then he dreamed another dream and told it to
his brothers and said, 'Behold I have dreamed another
dream. Behold, the sun, the moon, and eleven stars were
bowing down to me'" (ESV).

Traditionally, these eleven stars are interpreted to be
Joseph's brothers and the twelfth star as Joseph himself.
However, the image of the pregnant woman with a
crown of stars birthing Israel in Revelation 12 would
then not make sense, considering Joseph's dream dates
all the way back in Genesis 37. It would have best fit the
understanding of John's hearers that the pregnant woman
who was shrouded in sunlight, standing on the moon
with a crown of twelve stars, was an image of Eve giving
birth to faithful Israel. This woman who is wedded to
God is experiencing a great tribulation.

Even now, God is doing something with Israel. He
still maintains her as His chosen people. In Romans 9–
11, Paul emphasized God is not finished with Israel,
affirming this truth. Therefore, it is important to realize
the church has not replaced Israel; rather, the church has
been grafted in (see Romans 11:11–31).

The Red Dragon

John followed this image of the travailing woman giving birth and presented imagery that echoes prophecy in Daniel 7:

> *Behold, a great red dragon, with seven heads and ten horns, and on his heads seven diadems. His tail swept down a third of the stars of heaven and cast them to earth. —**Revelation 12:3–4 (ESV)***

The red dragon is none other than Satan, whose origins are extremely ancient. Ezekiel 28 says Lucifer (Satan's pre-fall name) was full of wisdom and beauty— a guardian cherub.[112] He walked in the Holy Place where God's throne stood, but his heart was filled with pride. Lucifer then launched a rebellion in heaven as a result of his pride—taking a third of the angels with him (see 2 Peter 2:4, Jude 6, and Isaiah 14). Satan and his minions have been wreaking havoc in both the spiritual and physical realms ever since.

John's description of seven heads with seven crowns signifies seven complete destructive rulers of the earth under the Dragon's control who are against Israel. The ten horns represent kingdoms that stand against God's people; the Dragon has been allowed limited authority over the earth.

A Cosmic Battle

John was describing the cosmic battle of good and evil. Satan, though it may appear he has power, is not all-powerful like God. Satan is a created being, is not omniscient, and he can't be in more than one place at one time. Because of this, the only perceived power he has is what God has allowed. Nonetheless, in Revelation 12:4, John described imagery of the Dragon's *attempt* to terminate God's plans:

> *And the dragon stood before the woman who was about to give birth, so that when she bore her child he might devour it. She gave birth to a male child, one who is to rule all the nations with a rod of iron, but her child was caught up to God and to his throne.* —
> **Revelation 12:4–5 (ESV)**

The woman was travailing in labor, and Satan was in place ready to devour her child to make sure it did not come into the world. Revelation 12:5 says the woman gave birth to a male child, one who would rule all the nations with a "rod of iron"; the child was caught up to God and to His throne.

Since the beginning, Satan has tried to eliminate the possibility of Jesus coming into the world. Many theologians refer to this as the "scarlet thread" of Scripture, the bloodline of the Messiah.[113] Throughout history, Satan has unsuccessfully tried to eliminate this line; he knew it would be through the bloodline beginning with Eve that he would meet his eventual destruction (Genesis 3:15).

In Genesis 6, the corruption of Adam's line intensified as intermarriages with the "daughter of humans" occurred and wickedness increased. The Jewish people were later attacked during Hezekiah's reign, when Sennacherib, King of Assyria, invaded Judah (see Isaiah 36 and 38). The bloodline almost came to an end.

Later, King Jehoiakim had a son, Jeckeniah (also known as Jehoiachin in 1 Chronicles 3:16 NIV), from the line of David. Jehoiachin angered God by burning one of Jeremiah's scrolls. God pronounced a curse on him, saying "Write this man down as childless, a man who shall not succeed in his days, for none of his offspring shall succeed in sitting on the throne of David and ruling again in Judah" (Jeremiah 22:30). True to God's Word, none of Jehoiachin's sons ever ruled as David did—but Joseph, Jesus' earthly father, was from Jehoiachin's line. Was God contradicting Himself? In Jeremiah, God had declared a descendent from the line of David would rise to the throne:

> Behold, the days are coming, declares the Lord, when I will raise up for David a righteous Branch, and he shall reign as king and deal wisely, and shall execute justice and righteousness in the land. In his days Judah will be saved, and Israel will dwell securely. And this is the name by which he will be called: 'The Lord is our righteousness.' — *Jeremiah 23:5–6 (ESV)*

Jesus was born of Mary and Joseph, and though Joseph's line had been cursed excluding him from being the genetic father of Jesus, Mary was born from the line of Nathan, one of David's other sons (see Luke 3:31). God's promise that Jesus would be born of the line of David was still fulfilled, as Mary was the biological mother of Jesus. The bloodline was preserved; the curse had been avoided through the virgin birth; Satan did not win.

Another example of Satan's attempt to destroy the nation of Israel was documented in the book of Esther. Evil Haman's plot to wipe the Jewish people out came to a halt because of one Jewish girl who stood firm for her people.

Satan attempted to use each of these people in the Old Testament to eliminate the promised Messiah; when the Messiah returns to this earth at His second coming, Satan's days will be numbered.

In the New Testament, when Herod learned from the Magi that the King of the Jews had been born, he attempted to kill him by murdering every male baby under two years old (Matthew 2:16). This bloody massacre was dubbed the "Slaughter of the Innocents,"[114] which hearkens back to Pharaoh's attempt to do the same just before the Israelite's exodus out of Egypt.

When Jesus was tempted by Satan in the wilderness to jump off the pinnacle of the temple to His death, Jesus overpowered him with the Word of God (Matthew 4:7).

Satan's continued attempts after Christ's birth to eliminate the bloodline were futile.

The Turning Point in History

But John next revealed a glimmer of hope!

And I heard a loud voice in heaven, saying, "Now the salvation and the power and the kingdom of our God and the authority of his Christ have come, for the accuser of our brothers has been thrown down, who accuses them day and night before our God. And they have conquered him by the blood of the Lamb and by the word of their testimony, for they loved not their lives even unto death. Therefore, rejoice, O heavens and you who dwell in them! But woe to you, O earth and sea, for the devil has come down to you in great wrath, because he knows that his time is short! — **Revelation 12:10–12 (ESV)**

Revelation 12:10 describes the moment of the cross—when Satan was conquered by the blood of the Lamb by the word of the believers' testimony, for "they loved not their lives even unto death" (Revelation 12:11 ESV). This was the turning point of history. The cross was God's ultimate victory—but the world still waits for Jesus to return and crush His enemy forever. Because of this, it is important for believers to know how to respond.

Satan knows he has been defeated—that "his time is short" (Revelation 12:12 ESV). John described Satan's continual attempts to defeat God, as well as God's protection of the woman, who is Israel:

And when the dragon saw that he had been thrown down to the earth, he pursued the woman who had

given birth to the male child. But the woman was
given the two wings of the great eagle so that she
might fly from the serpent into the wilderness. —
Revelation 12:13–14 (ESV)

In the Old Testament, a reference to eagle's wings was symbolic of the arms of God lifting up and protecting His people. Thus, in Revelation 12:14, John was describing God protecting His remnant: faithful Israel.

The serpent, however, continues to attempt to eliminate the woman:

The serpent poured water like a river out of his mouth
after the woman, to sweep her away with a flood. —
Revelation 12:15 (ESV)

John said the serpent tries to wipe Israel out with the waters of persecution. What he described next, however, is even more powerful:

But the earth came to the help of the woman, and the
earth opened its mouth and swallowed the river [of
persecution] that the dragon had poured from his
mouth. — Revelation 12:16 (ESV)

Victory over Satan is only because of Jesus and always because of Jesus. There will never be a new method or program to defeat Satan—it will forever be through the blood of Christ. Jesus alone has defeated the enemy, and it is in His blood that believers stand; it's that blood Christians celebrate in communion.

Overcoming

Most believers experience days where they feel defeated—as if Satan has accused them and he is right; they have "messed up" again. Believers often try to fix their mistakes by what is called willpower.

However, the first step of recovery happens when a person realizes life is out of their control, that they are *not* God, and they need help from something bigger than themselves. Believing one can do this by themselves—creating a religion of willpower—is self-worship.

How should the believer respond to a world fighting against everything they believe in? How can they overcome?

Victory can only happen with faith and hope, revealed through love. This should be the response of the church. Jesus did not teach that the world would know Christians belong to Him because of their big churches or inspiring programs that use the latest and greatest technology. The world would recognize them by the way they love each other (John 13:35). Overcoming and continuing to defeat Satan results when a believer trusts in Jesus Christ, and then shares their story. Satan, who has already been conquered, *continues* to be defeated each time this happens.

Christians share testimonies so that others hear *this is where I am, and this is what God did. If God can do that for me, He can do that for you.* This is true love for the other person, which instills hope.

In spite of his defeat, Satan continues to attempt to thwart God's plan:

> *Then the dragon became furious with the woman and went off to make war on the rest of her offspring.* — **Revelation 12:17 (ESV)**

Enraged, the Dragon battles the woman's offspring. The Jewish people are her offspring, but also the church—anyone who professes faith in Jesus. Satan will continue to war against faithful Israel whom God still has a plan for. History is moving toward the fulfillment of God's promises which will occur in the millennial kingdom when Jesus returns. Remain faithful and true and know God is still in control!

WORKBOOK

Chapter Seventeen Questions

Question: How does it make you feel to know the victory you have is all because of Jesus?

_____

_____

_____

_____

_____

_____

_____

_____

_____

_____

_____

_____

_____

Question: In what specific ways can the church respond with love in the face of hardships?

_____

_____

_____

_____

_____

_____

_____

_____

_____

_____

Question: How has God come to your rescue in a trial or time of suffering?

_____

_____

_____

_____

_____

_____

_____

_____

_____

_____

_____

_____

Question: Jesus overpowers Satan with the Word of God. How can you emulate Jesus in your life when you are tempted or struggling?

_____

_____

_____

_____

_____

_____

_____

_____

_____

_____

Action: The church has not replaced Israel, but has been grafted into Israel. Since the beginning, Satan has tried to eliminate the possibility of Jesus coming into the world, but the cross was the ultimate victory for God. Respond to temptations and trials in the knowledge that Christ alone has defeated all darkness.

Chapter Seventeen Notes

CHAPTER EIGHTEEN

Transformation in the World

The way to overcome and combat darkness, evil, and injustice is through faith, hope, and love. These are the primary weapons God has empowered the church with to fight this unseen battle. Christians should not retaliate in the way the world imposes its dominion narrative; followers of the Messiah should react and respond differently than the rest of the world.

God doesn't call believers to simply endure suffering and persecution—to sit back and take it without defending themselves. He calls Christians to transform darkness into light, pain into healing, and suffering into His glory. When Christians fight injustice and evil with compassion, mercy, and love, they topple Satan's dominion narrative and transform it into something utterly different. This is what changed an empire—it is how Christianity came to the forefront, from a persecuted church to a living, growing, empowered, and life-changing body of believers.

The church's task is to return to God's original call—to be the transforming agent of God in the world. It can do this only by extending grace and mercy to God's enemies and thus extending health. The church should operate differently than any man-ordained religious institution.

The Unholy Trinity

John next painted a picture of a disturbing beast in the first few verses of Revelation 13:

> *And I saw a beast rising out of the sea, with ten horns and seven heads, with ten diadems on its horns and blasphemous names on its heads. And the beast that I saw was like a leopard; its feet were like a bear's and its mouth was like a lion's mouth. And to it the dragon gave his power and his throne and his great authority. — **Revelation 13:1–2 (ESV)***

Revelation overflows with Old Testament imagery. The blasphemous names on the crown emerged out of the sea, much as the beast (or demon) Leviathan did in the Old Testament (see Isaiah 27:1). In the Bible, the sea is a picture of chaos, unbelieving humanity, brokenness, and darkness.

Daniel 2 and 7 discuss kingdoms that overtake the world in many ways. Daniel 2 describes an image of a statue of gold, silver, brass, and iron, with feet mixed with iron and clay. Gold was representative of the kingdom of Babylon, 606 B.C. to 539 B.C.[115]

This calls for a mind with wisdom: the seven heads are seven mountains on which the woman is seated; they are also seven kings, five of whom have fallen, one is, the other has not yet come, and when he does come he must remain only a little while. As for the beast that was and is not, it is an eighth but it belongs to the seven, and it goes to destruction. —**Revelation 17:9–11 (ESV)**

Five kingdoms have fallen: Egypt, Syria, Babylon, Greece, and Rome. But what about the one that hasn't come yet? For which kingdom is the world still waiting to arise? Who is the "king" coming to deal this ultimate destruction?

There are two layers to what John is seeing: the tangible, historical layer, and the spiritual, symbolic layer. This ultimate destruction is the literal fall of Jerusalem in AD 70 under Nero.

The first beast possesses something much larger than Rome; it is not merely a human being. John described one of its heads incised with a mortal wound, but this mortal wound was miraculously healed—resulting in the whole earth marveling at and subsequently following the beast into idolatry. Keep in mind that during this period of emperor worship, state and religion overlapped, which was why Christians experienced so much persecution. Those who rebelled and refused to worship Caesar as lord were executed. Jews were exempt from Caesar worship;[116] Romans knew from Jewish uprisings they held firmly to one God. Thus, the Jews didn't experience the same persecution as the Christians did.

> *And they worshiped the dragon, for he had given his authority to the beast, and they worshiped the beast, saying, "Who is like the beast, and who can fight against it?"* — ***Revelation 13:4 (ESV)***

The Son sustained a mortal wound and rose from the dead while the Father granted the Son all authority, all dominion, and all power.

Two Things Never to Bring Up at Dinner

Revelation 12 reveals Satan's attempt to stop the bloodline, but Revelation 13 exposes Satan's constant attempts to emulate God—mirroring Him, but in a dark, evil fashion. The beast claims divinity for itself because it wants to be worshipped; the cultural parallel points to more of that same emperor worship.

Satan has typically infiltrated two world systems in an attempt to twist people's idea of God: politics and religion. The first beast represents politics and the second religion. Keep in mind Rome, at the time of John's writing, was attempting to meld politics and religion into one overpowering entity. Satan perverted governmental and civic institutions that were ultimately designed to help people and manage power; he deceived those within those systems which evolved into political systems that eventually exerted power and pain. When that happens, oppression is the natural byproduct.

The founding fathers of Christianity separated the religious establishment from the machinery of government, recognizing tyranny could result when state and religious authority become one. Historically, the world has not dealt with power well—when a nation rules with an iron fist as Rome did, its people are negatively affected.

How should Christians respond to this today—and how did the ancient church respond? Revelation 13 reminds believers there is a red dragon behind every political entity in the world. Believers "do not wrestle against flesh and blood, but against the rulers, against the authorities, against the cosmic powers over this present darkness, the spiritual forces of evil in the heavenly places" (Ephesians 6:12 ESV)—for these spiritual forces are at work in the world and its political systems. It is paramount that Christians operate first and foremost in the power of truth, love, and grace, rather than in the power of the state.

Taken Captive

The prophet Jeremiah wrote in Jeremiah 15:2 that those who are destined for death must go to their deaths, and those who are destined for captivity must go into captivity. Consider John's next words, which sound quite similar:

> *If anyone has an ear, let him hear: If anyone is to be taken captive, to captivity he goes; if anyone is to be slain with the sword, with the sword must he be slain. Here is a call for the endurance and faith of the saints.*
> *— Revelation 13:9–10 (ESV)*

According to John, there is a greater story at work for those who submit themselves to the sovereignty of God—who trust Him in all things. Sometimes aspects of the government Christians live under are good, but often governments are impacted by corrupt leaders who desire selfish gain. John said those living under Roman rule in the first century were to respond in a profoundly different way to governmental leadership when it was evil. Rome might bring its weapons against believers, but Christians were not to raise weapons against it. The way of Christ was different—it required higher ethics, value, and purpose. Then and today, believers should respond with faith and perseverance.

By the time John wrote Revelation, the church was several thousand believers strong. Church history never documented the church taking up arms against Rome. On the contrary, the church held true to John's command: if anyone was taken captive, to captivity they went. Thousands of Christians stood in first-century Roman Colosseums facing certain death and said: "I will not bow my knee to Caesar, I bow my knee only to Jesus. Whatever comes, comes, but I belong to Him."

Where did that spirit go?

Twenty-first-century culture says, "I will fight for what's mine." Yet Jesus taught, "Greater love has no one than this, that someone lay down his life for his friends" (John 15:13 ESV). Jesus' words are the antithesis of the world system.

Satan perverts governmental systems. God's rule and reign, however, is radically different. Christians living faithful lives and who persevere change darkness into light, ashes into beauty, and brokenness into healing. One hundred thousand Christians were willing to give their lives for the glory of God for no selfish gain, expecting nothing for being martyred for Him, but only to be His child. *This* is the church that transformed the Roman Empire—as people watched and asked, "What is it these Christians have?"

This is how the church should respond today.

Church and State, Separately

Just before Jesus' crucifixion, in the garden of Gethsemane, Peter picked up a sword and cut off a Roman soldier's ear. How did Jesus respond? He healed the ear of the High Priest's servant and told Peter to put away his sword because "all who draw the sword will die by the sword" (Matthew 26:52 NIV). This is why the separation of church and state is a blessing. In some ways, the Christian church has allowed itself to be deceived by an ideology that encourages a unified church and state. Believers even fight for this. However, a Christian religious party is not what is needed. What *is* needed are Christians who serve in politics without aligning with one political party over another. When this happens, believers have fallen into Satan's trap, and the church loses its influence.

> *Then I saw another beast rising out of the earth. It had two horns like a lamb and it spoke like a dragon. It exercises all the authority of the first beast in its presence. And it performed great signs, even causing fire to come down from heaven to the earth in full view*

> *of the people. Because of the signs it was given power to perform on behalf of the first beast, it deceived the inhabitants of the earth. It ordered them to set up an image in honor of the beast who was wounded by the sword and yet lived. And it was allowed to give breath to the image of the beast, so that the image of the beast might even speak and might cause those who would not worship the image of the beast to be slain. — **Revelation 13:11–15 (ESV)**

It is likely John was referencing Caesar in Revelation 13:11–15. According to John, this second beast exercises all the authority of the first beast (in its presence) and forces the earth and its inhabitants to worship the first beast whose mortal wound was healed. This second beast performs great signs, even calling down fire from heaven. This second beast deceives those who dwell on earth—those who don't believe—and forces them to make an image of the first beast.

Scripture is clear: Satan's workers have always done his bidding—demons who perform pseudo-signs (such as the Egyptian magicians in Pharaoh's court who performed what *appeared* to be miracles). Today, dark magic and demonic arts are alive and well. There is a very real spiritual battle occurring in the unseen realm, manifested in what *can be seen* in this world.

In this spiritual battle described in Revelation 13, an unholy trinity mirroring the Father, the Son, and the Holy Spirit, stands against God and Israel. The Dragon is the father of darkness, and the Beast is his son. Finally, the breath of the Dragon that allows the beast to speak in Revelation 13:15 is the unholy analog to the Holy Spirit.

The Mark of the Beast

After this picture of a dark, evil, and unholy trinity, John plays with imagery again:

> *Also it causes all, both small and great, both rich and poor, both free and slave, to be marked on the right hand or the forehead, so that no one can buy or sell unless he has the mark, that is, the name of the beast or the number of its name. This calls for wisdom: let the one who has understanding calculate the number of the beast, for it is the number of a man, and his number is 666.* **— Revelation 13:16–17 (ESV)**

The Jews wore phylacteries on their foreheads and their arms.[117] The phylactery housed a little scroll; on this scroll was written the words of Exodus 13:1–10 and 11–16:

> *And it shall be to you as a sign on your hand and as a memorial between your eyes, that the law of the Lord may be in your mouth. For with a strong hand the Lord has brought you out of Egypt.* **— Exodus 13:9 (ESV)**

By wearing phylacteries, the Jews kept the law on their minds and hands, not only ideologically but in practice.

Recall the implications of receiving or not receiving the mark of Caesar. Without the mark of Caesar, people were not allowed to enter the agora—the marketplace.

John was referring to an imprint or seal—something that was real, but not completely literal.

Ideologically, the mark of the beast indicates that a person aligns with the Beast's teachings, his empire and dominion, and the famine, violence, and death that result. The character most scholars agree fits this number is the Roman emperor Nero. In Hebrew, *gematria*,[118] or numerology (which John's readers would have been familiar with, given the vast number of Hebrew references in Revelation), Nero's name equals 666.[119] John's numerical code would likely have used the Hebrew language rather than Greek or Latin to avoid detection from Roman authorities. Consider, too, that in Scripture, six is man's number; it is one short of God's perfect number, seven.

What It All Boils Down To

Satan knows Jesus is returning but doesn't know when; thus, he has prepared an unholy trinity in each generation. A "beast one" and a "beast two" are in the world right now, waiting for the return of Christ. This is why there have been rulers like Stalin and Hitler—each who have fit the job description of the Beast.

Be on the lookout for which world systems unite the political and the religious into a tyrannical reign; Satan is likely close behind, and because of this, the church should be watchful and ready.

WORKBOOK

Chapter Eighteen Questions

Question: How has the culture that says to fight "for what's mine" influenced you? What steps do you need to take to replace it with a biblical response?

_____

_____

_____

_____

_____

_____

_____

_____

_____

_____

_____

Question: What does living a radical life for Christ look like? How can you start walking in that direction?

_____

_____

_____

_____

_____

_____

_____

_____

_____

_____

Question: Where have you seen glimpses of the real, spiritual battle happening?

_____

_____

_____

_____

_____

_____

_____

_____

_____

_____

_____

Question: What are practical ways you can keep the law of God on your mind throughout the day?

_____

_____

_____

_____

_____

_____

_____

_____

_____

_____

Action: Satan is always trying to emulate God but in a dark fashion. Two things Satan uses to bring about darkness are politics and religion. Therefore, be alert to the temptation to rely on political or religious authority for salvation—or especially, to combine the two.

Chapter Eighteen Notes

_____

_____

_____

_____

_____

_____

_____

_____

_____

_____

_____

_____

_____

_____

_____

_____

_____

_____

_____

_____

_____

CHAPTER NINETEEN

The 144,000

When Jesus came to earth the first time, the Jewish people were hoping He would come with the scepter—as conquering King who would wipe out Israel's oppressors. But instead, Jesus came in love, peace, and as a servant. The second coming, which John spoke of in Revelation 14, is when Jesus will return to rule and reign. This is when everyone will stand before the Lord and make an account of their lives.

John opened Revelation 14 with an interesting statement about a unique group of people:

> *Then I looked, and behold, on Mount Zion stood the Lamb, and with him 144,000 who had his name and his Father's name written on their foreheads.* — **Revelation 14:1 (ESV)**

This number, 144,000, was first mentioned in Revelation 7, but in this passage, these "people" are being recast in another way. In Revelation 7, they were the sealed believers from all of time: believing Israel and the believing church. This number is derived from the twelve apostles and the twelve tribes, added together and multiplied by 1,000 (the number symbolizing an unmeasurable amount). This would lead us to understand the number as figurative and not literal.

Next, John described a voice thundering from heaven:

> *And I heard a voice from heaven and it was like the roar of many waters and like the sound of loud thunder. The voice I heard was like the sound of harpists playing on their harps, and they were singing a new song before the throne and before the four living creatures and before the elders. No one could learn that song except the 144,000 who had been redeemed from the earth.* — **Revelation 14:2 (ESV)**

John had described many other voices earlier in Revelation, but in Revelation 14, the voice John heard was louder and appears to be almost indescribable. The voice was singing a new song. Recall that each time God was victorious in the Bible, His people sang a new song. Whether it was after Moses and the Israelites crossed the Red Sea, or when Mary received the good news from Gabriel that she was with child—the response to God's work was to cry out in song. When a person is transformed because they put their faith in Christ and are added to the kingdom of God and written in the Lamb's book of life, believers celebrate. The proper response to Jesus' work in the people's lives is worship.

Pure Living

Unfortunately, the next two verses have caused much debate and disagreement because they are often misread:

> *It is these who have not defiled themselves with women, for they are virgins. It is these who follow the Lamb wherever he goes. These have been redeemed from mankind as firstfruits for God and the Lamb, and in their mouth no lie was found, for they are blameless.* — **Revelation 14:4–5 (ESV)**

If we read this literally, it might appear God doesn't condone marriage because the only ones who can sing the song are virgins and therefore unmarried. But a sweeping condemnation of marriage cannot be supported by Scripture. The image John portrayed is of people who have stayed true and pure, following the commands of God. They have rejected their culture's anti-God beliefs, and according to John, "are blameless."

Christians are called to be light, truth, and beauty in the midst of a world that believes the opposite. Jesus' lifestyle becomes the believer's lifestyle. To embrace this life, followers of Jesus must constantly reject the teachings and philosophies of the culture which are anti-God.

Being a Christian is not a Bible study or doctrinal check sheet. Rather, it is a radical choice to love people who hate you and to step into the margins with people who are unacceptable to society. It is making a firm, lifelong commitment to ensuring justice is done in God's name on this planet. It's vowing to live a lifestyle different than the anti-God culture of this world so that when people see believers, they are drawn to them because "There is something different about them." It is saying "yes" to Jesus. Something in and through the Christian should be visible to others; they are supposed to be marked by an overabundance of love, a reflection of the love of Christ.

When you feel pressure, when you feel pushed down, and when you feel kicked around—when your faith and your beliefs are ridiculed and mocked, and when the truths you have confidence in don't seem to align with what the culture teaches—Jesus said, "Follow me" (Matthew 4:19; see also Matthew 8:22, 16:24; John 12:26).

Those who choose to follow Him regardless of what other people, religions, or culture say have a new song to sing. They will see Jesus' face, and have the name of the Father and the Son written on their foreheads (Revelation 22:4).

The Long-Suffering Grace of God

A warning followed John's description of this loud voice in heaven.

> Then I saw another angel flying directly overhead, with an eternal gospel to proclaim to those who dwell on earth, to every nation and tribe and people. And he said in a loud voice, "Fear God and give him glory, because the hour of his judgment has come, and

worship him who made heaven and earth, the sea and the springs of water."

Another angel, a second, followed, saying, "Fallen, fallen is Babylon the great, she who made all nations drink the wine of the passion[a] of her sexual immorality." — **Revelation 14:6–8 (ESV)**

This warning was for believers, to tell all those who haven't connected with and aligned themselves with God what's ahead—and it's a dire warning of impending consequence. Western culture prefers the loving, comfortable aspects of Jesus, all of which are true. However, it avoids talking about God's demand for holiness. But God is clear: for every cause, there is an effect, and for every design, there is a designer.

Then another angel ascends in the air and says, "Babylon the great, she who made all nations drink the wine of the passion of her sexual immorality," is fallen (Revelation 14:8 ESV). John's hearers would have immediately known what John was referring to. The imagery John depicted was of Babylon—the Roman Empire—coming to its end.

God reigns, He is victorious, and Jesus is coming back again.

Two Judgments

And another angel, a third, followed them, saying with a loud voice, "If anyone worships the beast and its image and receives a mark on his forehead or on his hand, he also will drink of the wine of God's wrath, poured full-strength into the cup of his anger, and he *will be tormented with fire and sulfur in the presence of the holy angels and in the presence of the Lamb. And the smoke of their torment goes up forever and ever, and they have no rest, day or night, these worshipers of the beast and its image, and whoever receives the mark of its name." — **Revelation 14:9–11 (ESV)***

A day is coming where all people, believers, and unbelievers will stand before the Lord. John continued his letter with a discussion of not one, but two judgments. One is known as the judgment for believers in which everyone who has believed in Jesus stands before God to account for the things they have done. However, those good works do not determine whether the believer will spend eternal life in heaven or not. Jesus has redeemed every person, once and for all, who professes faith in Him as Messiah. This is why it is paramount the eternal gospel continue to be proclaimed.

For those who have chosen not to believe, who aren't written in the Lamb's book of life, a second judgment awaits. This second judgment will not occur until the end of the millennial reign (after Jesus has returned). This second judgment is known as the "great white throne judgment," which is "the final judgment prior to the lost being cast into the lake of fire" with Satan.[120]

This judgment wasn't originally intended for humans, but for spiritual beings who rebelled against God—which is why God, through Jesus, has been on a rescue mission. Because of Adam and Eve's disobedience and their subsequent fall from God's grace, every person who ever existed after them was headed to this eternal place of separation from God. Jesus' whole reason for coming to earth was to snatch people out of this terrible fate.

This day is coming, and Christians need to take that fact seriously and respond with urgency. Scripture says that "the smoke of their torment goes up forever and ever, and they have no rest, day or night, these worshipers of the beast and its image, and whoever receives the mark of its name" (Revelation 14:11 ESV). John was trying to paint a picture of something he hadn't personally experienced but was seeing in his vision—what it will mean for those who are eternally disconnected from God.

Revelation 14:13 follows with a call to believers, the enduring remnant of the saints—those who keep the commandments of God and their faith in Jesus: "And I heard a voice from heaven saying, 'Write this: Blessed are the dead who die in the Lord from now on.' 'Blessed indeed,' says the Spirit, 'that they may rest from their labors, for their deeds follow them!'" (Revelation 14:13 ESV). In just one verse exists two types of good news: the good news that God is dealing with evil and the good news that He will bring ultimate justice in the world.

Those who follow Jesus, however, will not have an easy journey:

> *Then I looked, and behold, a white cloud [the spirit, the Shekinah glory of God] and seated on the cloud one like a son of man, with a golden crown on his head, and a sharp sickle in his hand. And another angel came out of the temple, calling with a loud voice to him who sat on the cloud, "Put in your sickle, and*

reap, for the hour to reap has come, for the harvest of the earth is fully ripe." So he who sat on the cloud swung his sickle across the earth, and the earth was reaped. Then another angel came out of the temple in heaven, and he too had a sharp sickle. And another angel came out from the altar, the angel who has authority over the fire, and he called with a loud voice to the one who had the sharp sickle, "Put in your sickle and gather the clusters from the vine of the earth, for its grapes are ripe." So the angel swung his sickle across the earth and gathered the grape harvest of the earth and threw it into the great winepress of the wrath of God. — ***Revelation 14:14–19 (ESV)***

In John's vision, Jesus was trotting a winepress, an image that communicates the wrath to come for those who do not believe in Jesus. The cross is the answer to the wrath of God and salvation. According to Revelation 14:20, blood flowed from the winepress "as high as the horses' bridles" for 1,600 stadia (ESV)—that is, 160 miles.[121] That is an image of all who reject the Lamb and follow the philosophies of the world.

The writer of Hebrews said, "So Christ, having been offered once to bear the sins of many, will appear a second time, not to deal with sin but to save those who are eagerly waiting for him" (Hebrews 9:28). The Lamb has conquered sin through His blood; believers are called to follow Jesus no matter what the cost, enduring all things as they eagerly wait for His return—for the harvest of the first angel with the sharp sickle.

WORKBOOK

Chapter Nineteen Questions

Question: What is one example of someone from the Bible crying out in song to God that touches your heart? Why?

_____

_____

_____

_____

_____

_____

_____

_____

_____

_____

_____

Question: Christians are supposed to be marked by an overabundance of love. How then would you rate your current level of love? What is one way you can grow in practicing Christian love?

_____

_____

_____

_____

_____

_____

_____

_____

_____

_____

Question: Why is holiness important to God? How can you grow in holiness by the grace of God?

_____

_____

_____

_____

_____

_____

_____

_____

_____

_____

_____

_____

_____

_____

_____

_____

_____

Question: How can you more urgently proclaim the gospel to others? Make a list of ideas and select one to implement this week.

_____

_____

_____

_____

_____

_____

_____

_____

_____

_____

_____

Action: Each time God is victorious in Scripture, people sing a new song. God is dealing with evil and will bring ultimate justice in the world. Let your overabundance of Christlike love be evident to all!

Chapter Nineteen Notes

CHAPTER TWENTY

Persecution and Martyrs Today

Believers of the New Testament are to obey Jesus' words. Jesus taught His disciples to pray for and love their enemies, reminding them He had come to redeem the whole world. Jesus said if someone slaps you, turn the other cheek. If someone takes your shirt, give them your coat. (Matthew 5:39–40). The fullness of what these phrases indicate is hard to understand.

Christians are being persecuted to varying degrees across the globe. It may be losing a job because of faith in Jesus Christ or being mocked, or it could be the ultimate test of faith by losing one's life. Followers of Jesus will obey His words to love their enemies—even if that means showing love and kindness while being persecuted or attacked. John's vision described those saints who stood firm in their faith in the face of persecution.

As the third series of seven, this is going to be the completion or end of this story that we're going to see.

Seven Angels, Seven Plagues

Then I saw another sign in heaven, great and amazing, seven angels with seven plagues, which are the last, for with them the wrath of God is finished. I saw what appeared to be a sea of glass mingled with fire—and also those who had conquered the beast and its image and the number of its name, standing beside the sea of glass with harps of God in their hands. **— Revelation 15:1–2 (ESV)**

John mentioned this "sea of glass" back in Revelation 4:6 (see also Exodus 38:8, Ezekiel 1:18, 22). Both times John described the throne room of heaven, He said it was something like a sea of glass—likely, it was hard for John to put into words. But this time, John described this sea of glass "mingled with fire." Most often in the Old Testament (and even in the New Testament), fire was associated with God's judgment indicating this would be quite different from the beautiful tranquil sea of glass seen in Revelation 4:6. This time, the activity before God's throne will be judgment.

But John also saw what he described as "those who had conquered the beast and its image, and the number of its name," standing next to this sea of glass and holding harps (Revelation 15:2 ESV). These were saints who had been martyred for their faith, described with imagery of a river of blood.

Harps represent victory[122]—John's vision presented a different perspective of martyrdom. In the throne room of God, saints who had been martyred for their faith were standing, worshiping, and singing a song of victory.

The Song of Moses

This song of victory was called "the song of Moses the servant of God, and the song of the Lamb" in Revelation 15:3.

The song of Moses was a reference to the song of deliverance found in Exodus 15. The people of Israel sang this song after they had been delivered out of Egypt through the Red Sea which had supernaturally opened up to allow the nation of Israel to pass through safely. The waters had engulfed Pharaoh and the entire Egyptian army that had pursued Israel. The recipients of this Revelation letter would have been familiar with this song, as it was sung every Sabbath at Jewish synagogues.[123]

The song commemorates the greatest deliverance in Israel's history; how beautiful that John heard those martyred for their faith singing this same song praising God for deliverance! God has called His people in times of trouble to faith and perseverance, for He promises liberation will come.

Who Is Yahweh Moshe?

Deliverance is something God can't *not* do. Knowing who God is and what He does can be derived from knowing what His names signify.

Scripture reveals many different names of and descriptive terms for God which reflect His character—and one of His descriptive terms is *moshia'*. In English, this Hebrew word means *deliverer*. Thus, God is

Deliverer, which means "one who gives freedom from distress and the ability to pursue one's own way."[124]

Moshia' is derived from almost the same root word as *Moshe*, the Hebrew name for Moses. Notice the similarities: Yahweh Moshe—God who delivers—and Moses, the one who led Israel's deliverance from Egypt.

The entire Old Testament repeatedly called God's people to remember from whence they had been rescued—always pointing them back to their deliverance out of slavery in Egypt through Moses.

God is a God who is always delivering His people. Most people have been praying for deliverance from *something*; understand that God looks at deliverance, faith, and perseverance as things that will happen when God's people submit themselves to Him in faith.

Judgment and Justice

Judgment isn't often talked about in western churches; it's much more comfortable to focus on God's love instead. A common thought is the God of the Old Testament is a God of wrath, anger, and judgment; however, in the New Testament, he reflects love, life, and grace. The Bible is not two books, however, but one book with a common thread that runs from the beginning of Genesis to the end of Revelation: Jesus. God has not changed; He has been the same forever, which means He is still a God who rightly judges.

What happens when it seems people are not judged for their wrong acts—where cheaters don't seem to be held accountable, and thieves are allowed to run rampant? What happens when a government is corrupt and oppresses its people? Who do God's people have to cry out to?

God will one day judge all mankind; He hears those cries. Help and deliverance are on its way but will arrive in God's perfect timing, not man's.

Worship

God's judgment restores order. John said this would happen when all nations come and worship God for His righteous acts:

> *All nations will come and worship you, for your righteous acts have been revealed. — **Revelation 15:4 (ESV)***

God's judgment is a call for all people to worship Him—a vastly different definition than the world's typically negative view of judgment. Until that day, worship should be the believer's response to God's approaching good and fair judgment.

People have a choice to make. Psalm 58:11 puts it this way: "Mankind will say, 'Surely there is a reward for the righteous; surely there is a God who judges on earth'" (ESV). With this refined definition of judgment, does Psalm 58:11 rest differently in your heart and soul?

> *After this I looked, and the sanctuary of the tent of witness in heaven was opened, and out of the sanctuary came the seven angels with the seven*

*plagues, clothed in pure, bright linen, with golden sashes around their chests. — **Revelation 15:5–6 (ESV)***

John unfolds a peculiar picture next: the sanctuary of the tent of witness in heaven was opened. To understand the significance of what John saw, it's necessary to look to the book of Hebrews.

Hebrews 8 discusses the tabernacle God instructed Moses to build. The priests in that tabernacle, according to Hebrews 8:5, served in a sanctuary that was a "copy and shadow" of what is in heaven. This is why Moses was warned when he was about to build the tabernacle to see to it that he made everything according to the pattern God showed him on the mountain (Exodus 25:40). Thus, the tabernacle in the desert and later the temple (and everything within them) were intended to be constructed as copies of God's heavenly sanctuary. Thus, there is a place in heaven where God's law and mercy seat exist, and where God's glory dwells.

However, out of this heavenly sanctuary come "seven angels with the seven plagues, clothed in pure, bright linen, with golden sashes around their chests" (Revelation 15:6 ESV). John saw from God's heavenly abode angelic beings cloaked in symbolic clothing. They were donned in white linen, symbolic of priestly garments (see Exodus 28). The Old Testament priests served as mediators to the people, on behalf of God and representing God; these heavenly priests thus represented God to His people. Golden sashes adorned their chest, an indication of royalty—these angelic beings were representing the King. They were coming in full authority with a message from God, the King of heaven, regarding His eternal plan.

The Earth Surrenders

Four unique creatures interacted with these angelic messengers:

> *And one of the four living creatures gave to the seven angels seven golden bowls full of the wrath of God who lives forever and ever, and the sanctuary was filled with smoke from the glory of God and from his power, and no one could enter the sanctuary until the seven plagues of the seven angels were finished. —* **Revelation 15:7–8 (ESV)**

These creatures are the same four discussed in Revelation 4:

> *And around the throne, on each side of the throne, are four living creatures, full of eyes in front and behind: the first living creature like a lion, the second living creature like an ox, the third living creature with the face of a man, and the fourth living creature like an eagle in flight. —* **Revelation 4:6b–7 (see also Revelation 5:6–14, 6:1–8, 14:3, 19:4)**

These four living creatures represent the fullness of creation, indicating all of creation will play a part in whatever it is to come—the earth will surrender itself to God's plan.

Exodus 40:34–35 says, "The cloud covered the tent of meeting, and the glory of the LORD filled the tabernacle. And Moses was not able to enter the tent of meeting because the cloud settled on it, and the glory of the LORD filled the tabernacle" (ESV). Even Moses was not able to enter into God's presence in the tabernacle; he often entered the tent and pleaded with God on behalf of Israel, seemingly changing God's mind, so to speak. But once God establishes events in place, there is no one who can go in and ask God to change His mind. What God says is going to happen will happen; He declares in Isaiah 46:10, "My purpose will stand, and I will do all that I please" (NIV).

Mike Mason, author of *The Gospel According to Job*, wrote, "This is what faith is often like—do not be surprised if you find yourself confused, doubting, afflicted all but crushed. It does not mean that you have lost favor with God."[125]

Take heart and know God has overcome the world. Be strong in your faith even during trials and any persecution you may face, knowing that God, Yahweh Moshe, will deliver you.

WORKBOOK

Chapter Twenty Questions

Question: How is judgment a call to worship? How often do you talk about the judgment of God? How does such talk make you feel?

_____

_____

_____

_____

_____

_____

_____

_____

_____

_____

_____

Question: How have you seen God act as Deliverer in your life or in the lives of others you know?

_____

_____

_____

_____

_____

_____

_____

_____

_____

_____

Question: How does knowing God has a plan, and that it will be fulfilled, encourage your heart?

_____

_____

_____

_____

_____

_____

_____

_____

_____

_____

_____

_____

Question: Write about a time you experienced the presence of the Lord. How did it impact you?

_____

_____

_____

_____

_____

_____

_____

_____

_____

_____

_____

Action: God has called His people to faith and perseverance in times of trouble. God is always delivering His people. Surrender yourself to God's plan!

Chapter Twenty Notes

_____

_____

_____

_____

_____

_____

_____

_____

_____

_____

_____

_____

_____

_____

_____

_____

_____

_____

_____

_____

CHAPTER TWENTY-ONE

Revelation 16:
#NOTWHATYOUTHINK

Theodore Parker once said: "The arc of the moral universe is long, but it bends toward justice."[126] God is moving His plan toward ultimate and complete justice, but it is a long journey; sometimes in the wait, believers may feel justice will never come.

Deep within every person's soul, the voice of God sings songs about a different reality—a reality of an upside-down world turned right side up, the way things were intended. Jesus came to make all things new (Revelation 21:5), and His followers are an active part of that plan. Somehow, Christians have been deceived into thinking they must practice loving their enemies, accepting them wholeheartedly, which negates their ability to be angry at evil. This is incorrect thinking. God is holy and just, and He hates what has disrupted peace (*shalom*) and separated His people from Him. God is working all things together to restore that peace to its original place before the fall—and the absence of evil.

In his book *The Jesus I Never Knew*, author Phillip Yancey wrote:

> To believe in future rewards is to believe that the long arm of the Lord bends toward justice. To believe that one day the proud will be overthrown and the humble raised up and the hungry filled with good things. The prospect of future rewards in no way cancels out our need to fight for justice now, in this life. Rather, it allows us to believe in a just God after all. Like a bell totally from another world Jesus promises rewards proclaims that no matter how things appear, there is no future in evil, only in good.[127]

There is no future for evil—only in good!

The book of Revelation is an unveiling, a removing away of layers of what God has kept hidden for a time to assure God's children He is still in control. He does have a plan, and it is good. Above all, He is moving this plan toward its conclusion: justice will be His.

When the plagues enveloped Egypt, good still prevailed. Any Israelite who trusted God and placed the lamb's blood on the lintels of their house experienced God's protection; their firstborn sons were "passed over," or saved from death. John declared another greater Passover experience in Revelation 16; his vision looked forward to coming plagues which would not affect followers of God but would affect those who deny Him and who take the mark of the beast. In other words, those who preferred the world systems to God's system suffered judgment; however, God's wrath "passed over" believers.

John's revelation saw God's people rejoicing because eternal death did not swallow them up; this was the answer to the prayers that came from the altar in heaven.

Trusting God's Judgment and Breaking Down the Passages

John affirmed God's response to darkness and evil as he attempted to describe God's wrath poured out on the earth.

An angel emptied out his bowl on the land, and ugly festering sores broke out on the people who had taken the mark of the beast and worshipped his image (Revelation 16:2). Remember, the mark of the beast was an identifier of those who followed the imperial power of Rome which was powered by satanic activity.

Then, John described the activity of a second and third angel:

> *The second angel poured out his bowl into the sea, and it became like the blood of a corpse, and every living thing died that was in the sea. The third angel poured out his bowl into the rivers and springs of water, and they became blood.* — **Revelation 16:3–4 (ESV)**

Recall in Revelation 6:9 that John described martyrs slain for the Word of God as under the altar enthroned in heaven, waiting for God's vengeance; their voices cried out for justice.

God is not a capricious God. He is always good, and until a person understands this concept, they will never understand He is also perfectly just. Believers must release their right of vindication into God's hands for He is sovereign—this is no easy task. When a person trusts that God will make all things right and He is good, they will be released to forgive and as a result, experience peace (shalom) in their life.

> *The fourth angel poured out his bowl on the sun, and the sun was allowed to scorch people with fire. They were seared by the intense heat and they cursed the name of God, who had control over these plagues, but they refused to repent and glorify him. The fifth angel poured out his bowl on the throne of the beast, and its kingdom was plunged into darkness.* — **Revelation 16:8–10 (NIV)**

Despite a horrible plague of fire, those who denied Christ refused to repent and acknowledge God's authority. When a person acknowledges they have sinned and asks for forgiveness, God pours it out generously.

The fifth angel poured out his bowl on the throne of the beast, and "its kingdom was plunged into darkness" (Revelation 16:10 ESV). John described judgment upon the world's political system. Rome and its kingdom plunged into darkness; people gnawed their tongues in agony and cursed the God of heaven because of their pains and sores, but they refused to repent of what they had done.

There is no future for those who defy God's grace.

Christians Surrender … But Don't Always Surrender

When I first put my faith in Jesus, I came to the Lord selfishly; heaven sounded like a much more promising future than hell. Though I professed belief in Christ, I still defied God by trying to control my life.

Even after they have given their life to Christ, Scripture is clear believers must continue to crucify their prideful self—until the day they are face to face with God in heaven. This continual process of becoming more like Christ is known as sanctification. Paul wrote of this process to the church in Philippi exhorting believers to "work out your own salvation with fear and trembling, for it is God who works in you, both to will and to work for his good pleasure" (Philippians 2:12–13 ESV). Christians are redeemed from death to life the moment they believe in Jesus; however, they must work out their salvation continually.

Transformation is more than simply acknowledging the Word of God; it involves complete surrender to Jesus, which leads to submission to the Holy Spirit who takes over, leading and guiding the believer's life. At its essence, the transformation is the exchanged life Paul so powerfully speaks of to the Galatians: "I have been crucified with Christ. It is no longer I who live, but Christ who lives in me. And the life I now live in the flesh I live by faith in the Son of God, who loved me and gave himself for me" (Galatians 2:20 ESV).

Unfortunately, the church has embraced the idea that transformation occurs when believers keep a set of beliefs, theologies, and doctrines. However, this was not what Jesus taught; He said, "Follow Me." Only Jesus dwelling within a person can transform their life; the church's role is to come alongside the believer and gently and lovingly redirect their steps when they stray off course. Transformation has nothing to do with how good a person is, but rather how good *God* is.

Where Does God Make All Things Right?

Next, John described the satanic powers of world political and religious systems that convince people to deny God and follow the beast:

> *Then I saw three impure spirits that looked like frogs; they came out of the mouth of the dragon, out of the mouth of the beast and out of the mouth of the false prophet. For they are demonic spirits, performing signs, who go abroad to the kings of the whole world, to assemble them for battle on the great day of God the Almighty. And they assembled them at the place that in Hebrew is called Armageddon.* —**Revelation 16:13–15 (NIV)**

These demonic spirits that "looked like frogs" performed deceptive signs and gathered the kings of the whole earth to fight against God Almighty at a place called Armageddon.

But then, John paused between the sixth and seventh bowls.

Where does God ultimately put all things right?

Where will Jesus return to? *Jerusalem.*

I think what we are talking about is God dealing with all people in His holy city of Jerusalem. We're going to see at the end of Revelation, a brand–new Jerusalem; there is no future there for corrupt world powers

The scales of justice will come, and that's what the church was hearing because remember, Rome was just crushing the church. But God is saying to them, "Just remember that Rome is not on the throne, I am, and I will set all things right."

> *The seventh angel poured out his bowl into the air, and out of the temple came a loud voice from the throne, saying, "It is done!" And there were flashes of lightning, rumblings, peals of thunder, and a great earthquake such as there had never been since man was on the earth, so great was that earthquake. The great city was split into three parts, and the cities of the nations fell, and God remembered Babylon the great, to make her drain the cup of the wine of the fury of his wrath. And every island fled away, and no mountains were to be found. And great hailstones, about one hundred pounds each, fell from heaven on people; and they cursed God for the plague of the hail, because the plague was so severe. —*
> ***Revelation 16:17–21 (NIV)***

God is victorious, and declares "It is done!" It is as if John shifted to another camera angle to show what would happen at the end of all time. He wrote of flashes of lightning, rolling peals of thunder, and a severe earthquake—words indicating God had spoken. John described a quake so tremendous that the great city split into three parts and the cities of the nations collapsed.

God remembered Babylon the great and gave her the cup filled with the wine of the fury of His wrath.

Jesus declared, "I am coming like a thief (Revelation 16:15) and "I am coming soon" (Revelation 22:7). Though it might seem he is ahead, Satan knows his time is short. There is no future for corrupt world systems or those who defy God's grace. And there is no future for Satan. Things may not seem right today, but hold fast and know that God will make it right. God wins!

Chapter Twenty-One Questions

Question: How do you feel when you see injustice? How does knowing God will bring complete justice one day affect your perception of injustice?

_____

_____

_____

_____

_____

_____

_____

_____

_____

_____

_____

Question: When was a time you doubted God's goodness? How did God work in your heart to show He has always been good?

_____

_____

_____

_____

_____

_____

_____

_____

_____

_____

Question: How does a preference for the world's systems creep into your life? What are ways you can avoid preferring the world's systems to God's systems?

_____

_____

_____

_____

_____

_____

_____

_____

_____

_____

_____

_____

Question: What does surrendering to Jesus look like? What is one step you can take today to grow in surrendering your life to God?

_____

_____

_____

_____

_____

_____

_____

_____

_____

_____

_____

Action: Revelation is supposed to be showing you that God is in control, God does have a plan, and justice will be on earth. You can trust God's judgment to be right, true, and fair.

Chapter Twenty-One Notes

_____

_____

_____

_____

_____

_____

_____

_____

_____

_____

_____

_____

_____

_____

_____

_____

_____

_____

_____

CHAPTER TWENTY-TWO

Escaping Babylon

Revenge is an act of passion, but vengeance is an act of justice. Injuries are *revenged*; crimes are *avenged*. God requires His people to practice forgiveness because even vengeance—that is, justice—belongs to Him (Romans 12:19). He knows when His people involve themselves in seeking vengeance, they will mix it with their brokenness, creating an angry and often bitter longing for revenge. God, however, is holy, perfect, good, merciful, and loving when He judges. This was good news for Israel, a nation lost in the wilderness of sin, as Revelation 17 makes excruciatingly clear.

The Wilderness Escape

The wilderness theme often resurfaces in the narrative of Scripture, and Revelation is no different.

Then one of the seven angels who had the seven bowls came and said to me, "Come, I will show you the judgment of the great prostitute who is seated on many waters, with whom the kings of the earth have committed sexual immorality, and with the wine of whose sexual immorality the dwellers on earth have become drunk." And he carried me away in the Spirit into a wilderness, and I saw a woman sitting on a scarlet beast that was full of blasphemous names, and it had seven heads and ten horns. **— Revelation 17:1–3 (ESV)**

In the Bible, God often brought His people into the wilderness. In Hebrew, the word for wilderness is *midbar*, which means, "Pasture, uninhabited land, or a desert."[128]

The wilderness was a place noted for being apart from civilization; it was an in-between place of danger, temptation, and chaos, but also a place for solitude, nourishment, and revelation from God.[129] The wilderness became a metaphor for testing, judgment, refreshment, teaching, and empowerment. Consider a few examples:

- Abraham was brought into a wilderness that he didn't know to connect to God; he had only heard His voice.
- Moses was taken from the city into the deserts of Midian where he tended his father-in-law's flocks (Exodus 3:1). He would later return to Egypt, demand Pharaoh let God's people go (Exodus 8–10), and lead the entire nation of Israel out from Egyptian slavery and *back into* the wilderness—through the Shur desert—where God would meet their needs (Exodus 15:22–25).

- Jesus' ministry began in the wilderness, where He was tempted by Satan (Matthew 4:1–11). Though Satan attempted to convince Jesus to use God's power to do what he asked, Jesus responded each time with the Word of God. Jesus left that experience in the wilderness to go on to preach, "Repent, for the kingdom of heaven is at hand" (Matthew 4:17 ESV) and shortly after, called His first disciples.

When everything seems to be falling apart, trust God and avoid making life-changing long-term decisions. Embrace these "wilderness" times and allow God to minister to you and reveal Himself to you. He will begin to show you from an outside perspective what's really going on in your heart. The battle rages on, and it is paramount that you find clarity, vision, and refreshment—and sometimes to repent and seek God's forgiveness— to continue to fight strong.

The Mysterious Woman

The woman was arrayed in purple and scarlet, and adorned with gold and jewels and pearls, holding in her hand a golden cup full of abominations and the impurities of her sexual immoralities. And I saw the woman, drunk with the blood of the saints, the blood of the martyrs of Jesus.
— Revelation 17:4–5 (ESV)

The woman in Revelation 17:4 signified corrupt religious systems; John portrayed her as gorgeous, tantalizing, and seductive; she appeared religious, having the faith everybody seeks.

She held a golden cup full of "the impurities of her sexual immoralities," representing temptations that draw people away from true worship of God.

On the harlot's forehead was engraved, "Babylon the great, mother of prostitutes and of earth's abominations." Roman prostitutes often wore headbands embroidered with their names. This harlot was larger than any one branch of a religious institution—what theologian David Guzik described as, "The embodiment of Satan's own ecumenical movement—the religion of the world system."[130]

"Babylon the great" was a code name, identifying this woman as the source, or mother, of all idolatry and spiritual adultery—everything disgraceful on earth. John saw this woman, "drunk with the blood of the saints, the blood of the martyrs of Jesus" (Revelation 17:6 ESV); she persecuted the godly, reveling in it as a drunk takes pleasure in wine.

The angel next asked:

*Why do you marvel? I will tell you the mystery of the woman, and of the beast with seven heads and ten horns that carries her. — **Revelation 17:7 (ESV)***

Read the following list, which will reveal who this mystery woman is:

- This woman in Revelation has been called Sodom, Egypt, and Babylon.
- The woman is located where Jesus was crucified.
- The woman's dwelling becomes a river of blood, the woman is split into three divisions, the woman sits on the many waters (Revelation 17) and these waters are diverse people (17:15).
- The woman has fornicated with the heathen world and colluded religiously against God (Revelation 17:2, 18:3, 18:9).
- The woman is born on the beast (Revelation 17:3).
- The woman is the mother of all whores and abominable atrocities (Revelation 18:5).
- The woman is drunk on the blood of Old and New Testament saints (Revelation 17:6, 18:24, 18:20).
- The woman is responsible for the death of the prophets and apostles (Revelation 17:18).
- The woman sits on seven mountains (Revelation 17:9).
- The woman is a dwelling place of devils; the woman is a present for evil spirits (Revelation 18:2).
- The woman is a cage full of dirty birds. The woman has a full cup of iniquities. (Revelation 18:5).
- The woman is doubly judged (Revelation 18:8).

- The woman considers herself a queen (Revelation 18:7).
- This woman still considers herself married (Revelation 18:7).
- The woman was rich and mourned when she was judged (Revelation 18:10, 18:16–19).
- The woman merchandised the souls of men (Revelation 18:13).
- The woman has been "laid waste" (Revelation 18:19 ESV).
- The woman's sounds of joy are taken away (Revelation 18:22).
- The woman's capacity to produce and be industrious is taken away (Revelation 18:22).
- The woman's authority as someone equipped to judge is removed. The woman's light-bearing abilities are snuffed out (Revelation 18:23).
- The woman's bridegroom has divorced her (Revelation 18:23).
- The woman is called by the names of several great cities (Revelation 11:8, 14:8, 16:9, 17:18, 18:10, 16, 18, 19, 21, and 21:10).

Who is this woman?
Jerusalem.

Jerusalem was supposed to be the place that reflected the justice, mercy, beauty, and love of God to the entire world. Justice and peace were supposed to flow from within its gates. Because national Israel rejected her

Messiah, Jerusalem had become something utterly different.

Obviously, the woman was unrepentant—a character trait of the people of Jerusalem which was destroyed in AD 70. When the spiritual, economic, and political enmesh, the result is never good—John reminded his readers of this over and over in this letter.

C. S. Lewis said of all bad men, religious bad men are the worst.[131] Lewis was onto something. Throughout history, when religion grows powerful, it wounds people. Those with religious authority who have caused spiritual injury to others have broken and betrayed a sacred trust. Religious leaders should above all love and assist in healing others; when a religious leader embraces political power and economic systems to elevate their life, where do their followers go?

An Exodus People

Of all the people in the world, Israel knew what being enslaved to another nation was like.

> *And the merchants of the earth weep and mourn for her, since no one buys their cargo anymore, cargo of gold, silver, jewels, [other expensive goods] wheat, cattle and sheep, horses and chariots, and slaves, that is, human souls.* —**Revelation 18:11–13 (ESV)**

God's people were once slaves in Egypt, but He supernaturally freed them. The Israelites, therefore, were an "Exodus" people; they were called to participate in freeing others, not to enslave them. John looked at the city where God's people were supposed to be reflecting God's nature and instead of finding only what was good and true, he found slavery.

Unfortunately, modern society still practices slavery. Everything is spiritual, even modern politics and culture. Though it may not seem to be true, every decision made by leaders of this country is a spiritual decision—even how immigration is handled.

The believer is called by God to speak up for those who are marginalized, oppressed, who don't have a voice, and whose rights are being trampled. The church should be the loudest voice when people experience injustice. But, just like the woman riding the beast, the western church has been heavily focused on how *large* a congregation is, how many programs a church has, and what others outside the church walls think. God's people have strayed so far from His purpose—and in doing so, they have missed God's heart for justice.

Three Temptations Up Close and Personal

Henri Nouwen addressed Christian leaders in his book *In the Name of Jesus*.[132] Nouwen powerfully reframed the three temptations of Jesus (Matthew 4:1–11). He argued Satan's first temptation lured Jesus to be relevant by turning stones to bread—the temptation to *do* something, to *be* something. Most people long to be relevant. Everyone wants a significant church, a relevant pastor, and important ministries. People worship relevancy, and not only in the United States; it is a global mindset. There is nothing wrong with relevancy unless the importance a person or church seeks becomes their identity. This longing to be seen and lifted up has resulted in people and churches that have lost their way.

I remember when I was a young, twenty-one-year-old pastor and I thought I had the answers to every problem. I saw older pastors (in that day, older was over forty) as "over the hill" and "done." They should be headed out to pasture, I thought. Now, however, as I grow older, I realize how *irrelevant* I have become to the younger generation. This is not unlike the way of the world: a church might be considered relevant to some but not to others.

Fighting for relevancy is ultimately a fight for identity. However, only God provides a person's (or a church's) true identity; if identity is found anything other than Jesus, the person or the church will never be settled—rooted—in anything. It will adjust to the latest and greatest trend, like a chameleon.

Refuse the temptation to be relevant. Jesus combated temptation too and is not unaware of how powerful worldly lures can be. He could have turned stones into bread when Satan tempted Him, but He knew who He was and held fast to his mission. Do you know yours? Do you know *whose* you are? Have you attached your worth or identity to something other than God?

The cure for this longing for relevancy is contemplative prayer and meditation. Begin asking the Holy Spirit to reveal what you have tethered yourself to—what provides your identity. A good indicator of where you are drawing your identity is to consider whether anger results when something is taken away or lost. That thing might just be what you are basing your identity in.

Satan's second temptation lured Jesus to be spectacular. It is a common temptation today—and it feeds on the longing to be known, famous. Western culture has rapidly escalated to one focused on individualization: "Look at me, see me. I am great; I am awesome." YouTube has contributed to this problem; people want to be watched and recognized, to see how many "hits" they can acquire. They frantically watch to see how many "likes" they receive on social media. This, unfortunately, is Babylon.

Fight this temptation by holding onto the truth of what God says about you: you are beautiful, a son or daughter of the King. When a person's identity is rooted in this understanding, they know who they are.

Power was Satan's third temptation. He wanted Jesus to bow down to him, seducing Jesus with every kingdom, nation, tongue, and tribe—it will all belong to you, Satan coaxed.

People tend to gravitate toward power and control when they are weak in the art of intimacy and relationship. Those who have intimacy and relationship with God never lead from power or control, but rather from influence and love. People whose soul is so broken they are surrounded by unhealthy relationships scramble to get their way using power and control. This is a picture of the world, is it not?

What does it mean to be *in the world* and *out of the world?*

What does it mean to come out of Babylon?

It means resisting the temptation to be relevant. Christians belong to Jesus, and out of His overflowing love that dwells within them, they should seek justice, goodness, beauty, and mercy.

Resist the temptation to be spectacular or powerful, but point everyone to the One who *is* spectacular. Jesus is *the* famous One; He is *the* great one—powerful, spectacular, and stunningly relevant. The believer's job is to follow Him out of the wilderness, out of Babylon, and mirror Him who is already beautiful, just, and true.

Chapter Twenty-Two Questions

Question: Describe a time when God brought you into a wilderness. What was God's purpose in bringing you into that wilderness?

_____

_____

_____

_____

_____

_____

_____

_____

_____

_____

_____

Question: Where do you tend to turn for your identity? How can you grow in rooting your identity in Christ?

_____

_____

_____

_____

_____

_____

_____

_____

_____

_____

Question: Which of the three temptations do you struggle with the most: the temptation to be relevant, spectacular, or powerful? How can you combat this temptation?

_____

_____

_____

_____

_____

_____

_____

_____

_____

_____

_____

Question: What is one way you can be a part of freeing people? How can you take a role, regardless of how small it may feel, in bringing justice to this broken world?

_____

_____

_____

_____

_____

_____

_____

_____

_____

_____

_____

Action: The wilderness becomes a metaphor for testing, judging, refreshing, teaching, and empowering. Learn to avoid the temptation to be relevant, spectacular, and powerful. God's people are called to be a part of freeing people, not enslaving people. The church should be the loudest voice crying out in the street when people experience injustice.

Chapter Twenty-Two Notes

_____

_____

_____

_____

_____

_____

_____

_____

_____

_____

_____

_____

_____

_____

_____

_____

_____

_____

_____

_____

CHAPTER TWENTY-THREE

The Wedding Garments

A. W. Tozer wrote, "Let us be alert to the season in which we are living. It's the season of the blessed hope calling for us to cut our ties with the world and build ourselves on this one who will soon appear. He is our hope, a blessed hope enabling us to rise above our times and fix our gaze upon him."[133]

No matter what a person has done in their life, whether spectacular, relevant, or powerful—or perhaps they have simply been faithful with the small things—they should praise the Lord. This is the time to focus on hope—to remember what God has done and how He has brought them out of the wilderness to wait for the great moment of His return.

Giving Praise, All the Time, for All Things

After exhorting his readers to understand the mystery woman in Revelation 18, John heard the loud voice of a great multitude in heaven crying out:

> *Hallelujah! Salvation and glory and power belong to our God, for his judgments are true and just; for he has judged the great prostitute who corrupted the earth with her immorality, and has avenged on her the blood of his servants.* **— Revelation 19:1–2 (ESV)**

Once again, John noted heavenly worship in response to God's righteous judgment. He then redirected his readers' focus to a particular group of people participating in this worship:

> *The twenty-four elders and the four living creatures fell down and worshiped God, who was seated on the throne. And they cried: "Amen, Hallelujah!"* — **Revelation 19:4 (NIV)**

As the voice of one of the angels called out from God's throne, John understood clearly. God is supreme, even above Satan:

> *Praise our God, all you his servants, you who fear him, both great and small!* **— Revelation 19:5 (NIV)**

Some people have been dealt a hand that has been particularly hard, whether because of illness, death, or persecution. Sadly, sometimes something drastically evil has occurred in a person's life—and there may not be a clear answer for how to process the trauma. God is sovereign over the darkest evil; He will avenge everything that has come against those who follow Him. John affirmed this when he described who is ruling with all authority from heaven:

> *Then I heard what sounded like a great multitude, like the roar of rushing waters and like loud peals of thunder, shouting: Hallelujah! For our Lord God Almighty reigns. —**Revelation 19:6 (NIV)***

Jesus reigns as conquering King. "Hallelujah," which means "praise the Lord," is an imperative, a command. God commands the believer's soul to praise God. However, in this text, it is a *response* of worship— "Hallelujah, praise God!" These hallelujahs, the only four in the New Testament, serve a purpose: to announce a marriage feast—the second coming of the Son of God, the return of King Jesus. His return will be so glorious, so incredible, so amazing, and so beautiful that John noted *four* hallelujahs within Revelation 19 alone (Revelation 19:1, 19:3, 19:4, and 19:6).

The Biggest Party in History

Believers have two positions according to John in Revelation: a bride, as well as the guest, both who will attend Jesus' glorious wedding feast.

> *Let us rejoice and exult and give him the glory, for the marriage of the Lamb has come, and his Bride has made herself ready ... And the angel said to me, "Write this: Blessed are those who are invited to the marriage supper of the Lamb." And he said to me, "These are the true words of God."* — **Revelation 19:7–9 (ESV)**

As Christians eagerly anticipate the return of their King, they should also be preparing to be involved in the greatest celebration in all of history.

There were a number of steps to ancient Jewish weddings. The first step involved signing a contract at the betrothal. The bride or groom would meet their spouse, and an agreement was made—the two would be married. The agreement was signed, but the marriage wasn't sexually consummated yet. The groom would leave to go prepare a place for his bride. In that period, the groom would make sure everything was ready for his bride. Often the groom would add a room to his father's house

The third step was the wedding feast—a joyous party and procession. A Jewish wedding feast was and still is probably the grandest celebration in all of Israel. The groom finally arrived at an unannounced time and day to retrieve his bride who had been waiting expectantly. The extravagant wedding feast ensued. During the time while the groom was preparing a place for his bride, the bride was also preparing herself.[134]

When Jesus ascended to heaven, two men in white robes comforted His mourning disciples and declared Jesus would return in the same way he left (Acts 1:11).

Why would Jesus return? Because He is preparing a place for His bride, those who choose to follow Him (John 14:3). Until then, the bride—the church—should be doing everything possible to prepare for this great day! This means believers should be examining their hearts, souls, and lives to be ready for the Lamb's return.

As a pastor, I have performed at least 350 weddings—I've learned a thing or two about brides and grooms along the way. When I sit down with the groom at some point apart from the bride, I say, "I want to tell you the truth today. This wedding day—it is all about her. She has probably been dreaming about this day her entire life—reading, watching, and envisioning her dream."

Almost every wedding is entirely focused on the bride, but *this* wedding in Revelation is all about the groom. It is all about Jesus—the revelation of the Bridegroom, the King of Kings. It is not the unveiling of the antichrist, nor the unveiling of Satan's schemes. It is not the unveiling of some weird plan that God's people are supposed to mysteriously figure out with a Bible code. John's revelation uncovered the Christ.

Jesus loves His bride so much that He has prepared an indescribable wedding banquet to exceed any earthly wedding banquet. Of that magnificent day, the apostle Paul wrote:

> For the Lord himself will descend from heaven with a cry of command, with the voice of an archangel, and with the sound of the trumpet of God. And the dead in Christ will rise first. Then we who are alive, who are left, will be caught up together with them in the clouds

to meet the Lord in the air, and so we will always be with the Lord. —1 Thessalonians 4:16–17 (ESV)

When Jesus returns, the church will be caught up in the air with Him—those who have died as believers first, followed by those who are still alive.

The Gift of the Fine Linen

...and his Bride has made herself ready; it was granted her to clothe herself with fine linen, bright and pure—for the fine linen is the righteous deeds of the saints. —Revelation 19:7–8 (ESV)

Jesus' bride was clothed with bright, pure, fine linen, contrasting the seductive purple clothing of the prostitute who ruled the beast. John noted fine linen was "the righteous deeds of the saints" (Revelation 19:8). This beautiful fabric represented the holiness, purity, and beauty Jesus imparts to His followers. His righteousness covers His bride.

The bride didn't dress herself or work hard for her wedding clothes; fine linen was *put on her.*

When you said yes to Jesus Christ, He began to "clothe you." As you continue to take off the old self, Jesus continues to put on the new. When you submit your life to Jesus and he covers you with His righteousness, transformation ensues. Sadly, the church doesn't experience dynamic spiritual transformation because she too often tries to "fix the old dress" in her power.

Paul wrote that "He made Him who knew no sin to be sin on our behalf, so that we might become the righteousness of God in Him" (2 Corinthians 5:21 ESV). When Jesus imputes His righteousness on believers, a supernatural love begins to grow deep in the core of their souls. Rules and regulations have no place in Christianity. At the core of Christianity exists a love relationship, a uniting of God's people to His heartbeat that He might transform and free those who trust Him.

God loves you, holds you, rejoices with you on your good days, and bears you up on your bad days. As you wait for your Bridegroom, prepare your heart by drawing closer to God and dreaming of the most beautiful wedding feast you will ever be a part of. You are the bride!

Chapter Twenty-Three Questions

Question: How does knowing God will one day contend with all evil bring you comfort as you encounter evil in your life?

_____

_____

_____

_____

_____

_____

_____

_____

_____

_____

_____

Question: As you wait for Christ's return, what are some areas in which you need to become better prepared?

_____

_____

_____

_____

_____

_____

_____

_____

_____

_____

_____

Question: How have you seen Jesus at work in your life and transforming you?

_____

_____

_____

_____

_____

_____

_____

_____

_____

_____

_____

_____

Question: What description of Jesus from this chapter stands out the most to you? Why?

_____

_____

_____

_____

_____

_____

_____

_____

_____

_____

_____

Action: Scripture promises God will contend with evil. Jesus is preparing a place for you, His bride, and in turn, your job is to prepare for His return. Christianity, at the core, is a love relationship—be united to God's loving heart and let Him transform you.

Chapter Twenty-Three Notes

_____

_____

_____

_____

_____

_____

_____

_____

_____

_____

_____

_____

_____

_____

_____

_____

_____

_____

CHAPTER TWENTY-FOUR

The Millennium

Sometimes Scripture is confusing. Because of this, Christians often interpret the Bible according to personal belief. The various interpretations of Revelation are evidence of this practice.

It is easy to manipulate Scripture in this manner, but it is critical for believers to let Scripture speak for itself and see what God was communicating through each author. Be mindful of what Scripture meant to the author's original audience to accurately interpret what it means for believers today.

The Millennial Reign of Christ

After John discussed the magnificent wedding feast of the Lamb in Revelation 19, he then presented the terrible fate of the Dragon:

> Then I saw an angel coming down from heaven, holding in his hand the key to the bottomless pit and a great chain. And he seized the dragon, that ancient serpent, who is the devil, or Satan, and bound him for a thousand years. — **Revelation 20:1–2 (NIV)**

John said the Dragon—Satan—would be bound for one thousand years—a new concept in John's letter. In theology, this period of time is also called "the millennium," or "the millennial reign of Christ." Millennium simply means *one thousand.*

When Jesus returns, Scripture makes known He is going to rule and reign over the earth for one-thousand years. But as previously discussed, few numbers point to actual, literal numbers in Revelation.

Was John envisioning a literal one thousand years or a symbolic number? The number three, the number seven, and the number ten (and its multiples, including one thousand) indicate completeness or fullness in the Bible.[135] Thus, John could have meant Satan would be bound for a literal one thousand years. Or, it could mean some specified complete period of time. Either interpretation would be in complete agreement with the way John has used the numbers throughout his letter.

Many opinions surround the millennial reign of Christ. When interpreting the Bible, it is crucial the student not hold too tight to one system of theology; rigidly holding one position often leads to forcing a text to fit that interpretation. *All* Scriptures must work together theologically, or misinterpretation is bound to occur.

Whether it's a literal one thousand years or a figurative period of time, Satan will nonetheless be bound for the duration. He will be thrown into the abyss—and the bottomless pit will be sealed.

Contemplate the different eschatological (end-times) views below.

Pre-millennialism. Many evangelical churches embrace a pre-millennial eschatological view. Pre-millennialists believe there is a millennial period of a literal one thousand years when believers will reign and rule with Jesus over the earth. During that time, faithful Israel will receive the promised inheritance of all the covenants from the Old Testament; she will receive the land promised to her in Genesis 12:1–7. Jesus will return and establish His kingdom before the millennium starts.

There are two different camps within premillennialism. First is *historical pre-millennialism* or the belief we entered the era of the tribulation after the ascension of Christ and the destruction of the temple in 70 AD. The church was faithfully waiting and preparing itself for His second coming. When Jesus comes, believers who are still alive will be raptured; those who have already died will be raised up first, and then raptured.

The other camp within pre-millennialism is *dispensationalism.* Traditionally, dispensationalism views the events in Revelation as happening in the future. Dispensationalism came about in the 1800s. John Nelson Darby was the first person to start teaching dispensationalism.[136] According to dispensationalism, all events in Revelation occur during a seven-year period, the fulfillment of Daniel's seventieth week from the prophecy of Daniel 9. After this literal seven-year period begins (a date unknown to any man), Jesus will secretly rapture His church out, either at the beginning of that tribulation period, in the middle, or at the end.

Dispensationalism has a strong following because of books like the *Left Behind* series by Tim LaHaye and Jerry B. Jenkins.

I believe the tribulation period is occurring now and believers are waiting for Jesus to return. When He comes for His bride, those believers who are still alive will see Him and be caught up with Him (see 1 Thessalonians 4:16–17). He will then establish His millennial reign. Be aware: Christians hold strong convictions regarding eschatological beliefs, but none are salvific. Brothers and sisters in Christ can hold any view of this mini-arena of Christ; what is important is that Jesus returns in all.

A-millennialism. A-millennial means there is no literal millennial reign; Jesus' kingdom is here now through the activity of the church. A-millennialists believe the thousand years to be a spiritual reign where the church rules and reigns through Christ dwelling within each individual believer. The church will experience both hard and good times during this time. Jesus will return on some unknown day.

Post-millennialism. Post-millennialists view the millennial period as a figurative thousand years where the church realizes the return of Jesus. Thus, the church is currently pushing back evil and darkness and the millennium will be its "golden age." During this time, the church will become all-powerful. Prior to the 1800s, this was a predominant view. However, this view poses a problem; the church was supposed to be making the world better, but it wasn't. Because of this, post-millennialism gave way to premillennialism.

Post-millennialism and A-millennialism embrace what is known as replacement theology. Replacement theology believes the church has replaced Israel. Because Israel did not believe in Jesus at His first advent, God has imparted everything promised to Israel in the Old Testament to the church; He is done working with national Israel.

Yet the book of Revelation is clear: God is *not* finished with Israel. He has a wonderful purpose and plan for His people.

Is it important to understand these views? Yes. What a person believes regarding the return of Christ should matter to Christians because a person's beliefs dictate their behavior. Their eschatological (end-times) view will affect their Christian witness and ultimately, life.

I have encouraged dispensationalists and premillennialists to be extremely careful and guard themselves against developing a pessimistic attitude. I have seen pre-millennial dispensational believers care nothing for the environment because they truly believe everything material will one day burn.

At the end of the day, Christians must rely on the words of Jesus who warned: "But concerning that day and hour no one knows, not even the angels of heaven, nor the Son, but the Father only" (Matthew 24:36 ESV). The Father will let Jesus know when it's time for Him to come back. Jesus doesn't even know when He is coming back.

So What Happens During Those Thousand Years?

In Revelation 20, John wrote to believers that Jesus would one day capture the great Dragon (Satan) who will be thrown into the abyss where he will remain for one-thousand years. During that time, the nations will experience peace—until the Dragon is released for a little while.

> *And when the thousand years are ended, Satan will be released from his prison and will come out to deceive the nations that are at the four corners of the earth, Gog and Magog, to gather them for battle; their number is like the sand of the sea.* — **Revelation 20:7–8 (ESV)**

John declared in Revelation that though Satan has had some freedom, he isn't sovereign. For some reason known only to the Father, after Jesus establishes His millennial kingdom—whatever God's fullness of time is— Satan will be released for an unspecified period of time.

Revelation 20:4 gives readers a hint of what's to come. John wrote:

> *I saw thrones on which were seated those who had been given authority to judge. And I saw the souls of those who had been beheaded because of their testimony about Jesus and because of the Word of God. They had not worshipped the beast or its image and had not received its mark on their foreheads or their hands. They came to life and reigned with Christ a thousand years.* — ***Revelation 20:4 (NIV)***

The dead in Christ will be raised—this is called the first resurrection, and believers in Christ are part of that. If you are alive when Jesus returns you will be caught up; if you aren't, you will be raised. And when Jesus returns, the judgment you will face will be different than the "lake of fire" judgment described at the end of Revelation 20.

There are two judgments in the Bible, and it's important to understand the difference in each.

The Bema Seat Judgment. This judgment is only for those who belong to Jesus. Followers of Jesus will be judged for the good works they have done and receive rewards that will remain with them into heaven. The way a person lives their life today, the way they serve and sacrifice for God, will be rewarded.[137] Remember, Jesus said, "Where your treasure is, there your heart will be also" (Matthew 6:21 ESV).

Consider work done today as an investment in the kingdom; invest in "treasures in heaven, where neither moth nor rust destroys" (Matthew 6:20 ESV). Prepare for when the Bridegroom returns and for what is ahead.

The Great White Throne Judgment. This judgment will occur at the *end* of the millennial reign for those who continually defied God. This judgment was designed for Satan and his angels, and unfortunately, the only other people who will be there will be those who followed the lies of the enemy.

Eternity is a long time, so follow hard after Jesus to fulfill the great commandment to "love your neighbor as yourself" (Mark 12:31 ESV). Choices in this life will carry to the next.

The call to live a life aligned with Jesus is not just a moral checklist—it impacts life in eternity.

The Two Most Important Words in the Bible

"So what do you think about heaven and hell? What do you think happens after you die?" When I ask this question of non-believers, most of the time they sheepishly answer "I think there is a heaven and a hell." They then say, "I am just hoping when I stand before God and His scales that my good pile is better than my bad pile. I'm a pretty good person; I haven't killed anybody."

My heart rips open every time I hear this answer.

Revelation 20 is clear: no person, no matter how amazing, good, or kind they are, has ever done enough to warrant eternity with God who is perfect. Heaven is where God dwells. When heaven and earth come together, and man and God dwell together, there will no longer be sin. Nothing unholy or untrue can dwell in

God's presence. I know I am not holy even on my best day.

When I said yes to Jesus when I was eighteen years old, He covered me in His holiness. He started preparing me for the great wedding banquet so that when He comes, I will not be worrying about what I am wearing because I am *in Christ.*

These two words—in Christ—are quite possibly the two most important words in the New Testament.

The consequences are dire for those who are not.

Don't Forget to RSVP

In Randy Alcorn's book *50 Days of Heaven,* Alcorn shared a story about a friend of his named Ruthanna Metzgar who was a professional singer. In the book, she was asked to sing at a wealthy man's wedding reception held at the Northwest's tallest skyscraper. You can just imagine how lavish this grand event was with servers in tuxedos. After a time of festivities, the wedding feast was about to begin. Ruthanna and her husband waited eagerly to enter, but there was a problem.

A gentleman with a lovely bound book greeted us as we reached the top of the stairs. "May I have your name please?" "I am Ruthanna Metzgar, and this is my husband, Roy Metzgar," I replied. The gentleman searched the Ms. "I'm not finding it. Would you spell it please?" I spelled it slowly and clearly. After searching throughout the book, the gentleman looked up and said, "I'm sorry, but your name is not here. Without your name in this book, you cannot attend this banquet." "Oh, there must be some mistake," I replied. "I am the singer. I sang for this wedding!" The gentleman calmly answered, "It doesn't matter who you are or what you did, without your name in the book you cannot attend this banquet."

Ruthanna had stood there dumbfounded watching the other guests enter the exquisitely-decorated banquet room with delicious smells escaping. You can sympathize with her when the attendant had her and her husband escorted out because they had no reservation. Later when her husband asked her what happened, she replied: "When the invitation arrived for the reception, I was very busy and I never bothered to return the RSVP. Besides, I was the singer; surely I could go to the reception without returning the RSVP!"[138]

Don't be too busy to respond to Jesus' invitation. Don't presume the good things you have done or your perfect church attendance will get you to heaven. Believe in Him, and accept His forgiveness for your sins.

WORKBOOK

Chapter Twenty-Four Questions

Question: Which millennial reign position do you believe? Why?

_____

_____

_____

_____

_____

_____

_____

_____

_____

_____

_____

Question: Think back to when you first became a believer. What is a prayer of thanks you can offer God for saving you?

_____

_____

_____

_____

_____

_____

_____

_____

_____

_____

Question: How can you respond to someone who is counting on his or her good outweighing the bad on judgment day? What questions can you ask to help this person think more deeply about salvation?

_____

_____

_____

_____

_____

_____

_____

_____

_____

_____

_____

Question: How can you grow in sharing your faith with non-believers and communicating the importance of being in Christ? Make a list of ideas and then select one you would like to try this week.

_____

_____

_____

_____

_____

_____

_____

_____

_____

_____

_____

_____

Action: Jesus returns and throws Satan into the bottomless pit until His reign is complete. There are two judgments, one for those who belong to Jesus and one for those who have defied God. Make sure you are in Christ, and ground your confidence in Him.

Chapter Twenty-Four Notes

_____

_____

_____

_____

_____

_____

_____

_____

_____

_____

_____

_____

_____

_____

_____

_____

_____

_____

_____

_____

_____

_____

_____

_____

CHAPTER TWENTY-FIVE

Describing Heaven

C. S. Lewis, in his book *The Last Battle*, described entrance to heaven this way: "I have come home at last! This is my real country! I belong here. This is the land I have been looking for all my life, though I never knew it till now; come further up come further in."[139]

And Steve Jobs, though grounded in secular and non-Christian worldviews, had this insight to offer about death and heaven when he delivered the commencement speech to Stanford in June 2005: "No one wants to die. Even people who want to go to heaven don't want to die to get there. And yet death is the destination we all share. No one has ever escaped it. And that is as it should be because death is very likely the single best invention of life; it is life's change agent. It clears out the old to make way for the new."[140]

As Jobs suggested, the death of the old leads to renewal; but as Lewis knew, heaven is the new that replaces the old. Heaven is indeed the way things ought to be—where believers *long* to be. Heaven is home.

Making All Things New

What John saw next is what the believer is waiting for:

> Then I saw a new heaven and a new earth for the first heaven and the first earth had passed away and the sea was no more. — **Revelation 21:1 (NIV)**

Christians often believe the earth is like a slum and believers are waiting for a heavenly existence in a completely different location from earth. However, God's plan revealed in Scripture indicates heaven will pick up where God started the journey; heaven and earth will be combined into one where God's glory—His presence—will radiate every square inch of this place known as eternity. This eternity will be heaven merging with earth, but it will be new.

John saw a new heaven and a new earth. They came together because the first heaven and the first earth passed away just like when a person believes in Jesus. Second Corinthians 5:17 declares the old has gone and the new has come—often termed "regeneration."

A new believer looks the same externally—but they are spiritually and internally a new creature. This is where God leaves a bit of mystery. In the same way, earth will still be earth, but it will somehow be renewed.

Regeneration has come to renew what sin has marred. This includes everything in the entire universe system.

> *Then I saw a new heaven and a new earth, for the first heaven and the first earth had passed away, and there was no longer any sea. I saw the Holy City, the new Jerusalem, coming down out of heaven from God, prepared as a bride beautifully dressed for her husband.* **— Revelation 21:1–2 (NIV)**

This should be familiar wedding banquet imagery, for John compared the New Jerusalem to a beautifully dressed bride—awaiting her bridegroom. Then, John proclaimed the heartbeat of the book of Revelation:

> *And I heard a loud voice from the throne saying, "Look! God's dwelling place is now among the people, and he will dwell with them. They will be his people, and God himself will be with them and be their God."* **— Revelation 21:3 (NIV)**

The earthly battle between good and evil has been a chaotic kingdom struggle for millennia. Now, John describes the Trinity's permanent invasion of earth.

Throughout Israel's history, each time God tried to "tabernacle" or dwell with His people, they cried out for another king—an earthly king. "Appoint for us a king to judge us like all the nations," Israel demanded (1 Samuel 8:5 ESV). God conceded, telling Samuel, "Obey the voice of the people … they have rejected me from being king over them" (1 Samuel 8:7 ESV). Israel was clear: her people did not want God to be king.

But John said when this New Jerusalem comes down to earth, "They will be his people, and God himself will be with them and be their God" (Revelation 21:3 ESV). God will finally be Israel's King. Seated on the throne, God the Father spoke: "Behold I am making all things new. Write this down. These words are trustworthy and true" (Revelation 21:5 ESV).

Think back to the seven churches discussed at the beginning of Revelation—churches under Rome's domination and experiencing horrible and daily persecution. People lost their lives. Hope was dampened, and faith challenged. For these first-century believers, Jesus' words at the end of John's letter declaring, "I am making all things new" (Revelation 21:5 ESV), must have carried so much comfort, hope, and power.

The world's current system operates on money. Imagine a world where no money is needed to enjoy activities, to purchase food. It will be a world where people will exist to bless others with the things they create and the things they purpose. John wrote, "The one who conquers will have this heritage, and I will be his God and he will be my son (Revelation 21:7 ESV). God *will* be King.

In this new, heavenly Jerusalem, something will be absent:

But nothing unclean will ever enter it, nor anyone who does what is detestable or false, but only those who are written in the Lamb's book of life. — **Revelation 21:27 (ESV)**

Nothing will exist in God's kingdom that is against Him, nothing "detestable and false." Only those written in the Lamb's book of life will be present; those who denied God will have been sent to the great lake of fire along with Satan and his angels. The lake will be gone, however; in God's newly-created order, in His presence, it cannot exist.

Heaven will be even better than anyone could ever imagine.

The Ultimate WOW Moment

*One of the seven angels who had the seven bowls full of the seven last plagues came and said to me, "Come, I will show you the bride, the wife of the Lamb." And he carried me away in the Spirit to a mountain great and high, and showed me the Holy City, Jerusalem, coming down out of heaven from God. It shone with the glory of God, and its brilliance was like that of a very precious jewel, like a jasper, clear a crystal. — **Revelation 21:9–11 (NIV)***

One of my most treasured moments from each wedding I officiate is standing center-stage with the groom who knows his bride is about to arrive. When she appears, everyone stands and all eyes turn to see the one her groom is waiting for. She is *the bride.* I love to watch the groom's reaction, which when he sees her beauty, is usually, *"Wow!"*

The angel was excited to show John the bride—as if to say, "John, *you have to see her, she's about to come down the aisle, and she is absolutely stunning!"* The angel carried John away in the spirit to a high mountain and showed him the holy city of Jerusalem, coming down out of heaven. Jerusalem was radiant, and the "dress" she wore was the beauty and the glory of God.

All things will one day come together and become one—imagery that echoes the beginning of the Bible—a man and a woman in a beautiful garden absent of sin, a husband and a wife, two flesh becoming one.

In this New Jerusalem, there will be oneness as the body of Christ: "There is neither Jew nor Greek, there is neither slave nor free, there is no male and female" (Galatians 3:28 ESV).

This oneness will be as intimate as the oneness between the Trinity: three persons constituting one God.

This new city will be filled with God's people, everyone who belongs to the Lord:

> It had a great, high wall with twelve gates, and with twelve angels at the gates. On the gates were written the names of the twelve tribes of Israel. There were three gates on the east, three on the north, three on the south and three on the west. The wall of the city had twelve foundations, and on them were the names of the twelve apostles of the Lamb. — **Revelation 21:12–14 (NIV)**

Paul wrote that the church has been grafted into Israel (see Romans 9–11), and the dividing wall of hostility had been destroyed (Ephesians 2:14). In the New Jerusalem, this oneness of people will fulfill Paul's words to perfection. Those who belong to God will be reconciled to Him and to each other.

And the one who spoke with me had a measuring rod of gold to measure the city and its gates and walls. The city lies foursquare, its length the same as its width. And he measured the city with his rod, 12,000 stadia. Its length and width and height are equal. —
Revelation 21:15–16 (ESV)

When these numbers in Revelation 21:15–16 are added, the city appears to be a perfect cube. And this perfectly-shaped city is constructed with exquisite materials John found hard to describe:

The wall was built of jasper, while the city was pure gold, like clear glass. The foundations of the wall of the city were adorned with every kind of jewel. —
Revelation 21:18–19 (ESV)

Precious stones existed in the garden, but this will be a *renewed* Eden—a new and improved paradise. Here there will be no more deception, brokenness, or sin, but only shalom peace and beauty. John wrote there would be no need for a temple because *God's presence is there* (Revelation 21:22). His glory will be everywhere—not confined to one place—and the New Jerusalem will be the centerpiece. Its "temple" will be God Almighty and the Lamb.

And the city has no need of sun or moon to shine on it, for the glory of God gives it light, and its lamp is the Lamb. By its light will the nations walk, and the kings of the earth will bring their glory into it, and its gates will never be shut by day—and there will be no night there. They will bring into it the glory and the honor of

> *the nations. But nothing unclean will ever enter it, nor anyone who does what is detestable or false, but only those who are written in the Lamb's book of life. —*
> **Revelation 21:23–27 (ESV)**

The New Jerusalem will have no need for the sun or moon for the glory of God will provide light—and its lamp will be the Lamb. What a beautiful picture of the Trinity!

The nations will walk by this light, and darkness will be non-existent.

Within this renewed city, heavenly worship will bring about healing. When God's people worship, His presence inhabits the praise of His people (Psalm 22:3). Where His presence is, His power is present, too. With God's power comes His ability to heal, to restore, to save, and to move.

When a believer enters into worship, God's power indwells them, too—they have His ability to heal, restore, save, and move. This power is missing in the modern church.

John ended his letter as if he were running out of words—there was no way to describe the beauty God had allowed him to see. He saw no more pain, no more sickness, no more tears, and no more death. He concluded his letter with the Lord's words of comfort—Jesus' last words to the church:

> *And behold, I am coming soon. Blessed is the one who keeps the words of the prophecy of this book. ... Behold, I am coming soon, bringing my recompense with me, to repay each one for what he has done. I*

am the Alpha, I am the Omega, the first and the last, the beginning and the end. ... The Spirit and the Bride say, "Come." And let the one who hears say, "Come." And let the one who is thirsty come; let the one who desires take the water of life without price. — **Revelation 22:7, 12, 17 (ESV)**

The new heaven and earth will be a new Eden—a new reality and a renewed creation where heaven and earth will be merged into one here, on a renewed earth.

Believers are not waiting to be transferred to a different place; no, God will one day renew all things, and it will be a physical, tangible eternity beyond anyone's ability to imagine.

Let us find our hope in these powerful words:

He who testifies to these things says, "Surely I am coming soon." — **Revelation 22:20 (ESV)**

Chapter Twenty-Five Questions

Question: How would you try to describe the heavenly existence to come? Write a note of praise to God for what is to come.

_____

_____

_____

_____

_____

_____

_____

_____

_____

_____

_____

Question: What misconceptions have you, or those you know, held about heaven?

_____

_____

_____

_____

_____

_____

_____

_____

_____

_____

_____

Question: How would you describe the mystery of 2 Corinthians 5:17 (the old has gone and the new has come) to a non-believer?

_____

_____

_____

_____

_____

_____

_____

_____

_____

_____

_____

Action: No one, not even John, can come close to describing what awaits those who belong to the Lamb. God's plan has always been for heaven and earth to be combined into one, and for His glory in His presence to radiate through every square inch of the new Eden. Don't merely wait to be ejected from this life into a better existence; instead, maintain hope and joy that God will make all things new.

Chapter Twenty-Five Notes

CONCLUSION

"I Will Make Everything New"

When I think about how to describe heaven, I think of a couple of my trips.

I remember my first to Uganda when I met my World Vision sponsored child and his family. We traveled along bumpy, dusty paths until we arrived at their dwelling in the midst of lush vegetation. On my second trip to Uganda a couple years later, my sponsored child, Baguma, and his father, Ibrahim, knew I was coming. As my team pulled into the village of Kasitu, Ibrahim and Baguma were there waiting for me with infectious smiles on their faces. They were so excited! They said, "We have a new home, and we want to show you!"

He led us to his house, with walls of mud, a floor of dirt, no running water, no electricity, and kids everywhere. We sat outside his house talking and sharing stories; it was a beautiful experience. Then he asked me this common question: "So, tell me about your house?"

Another trip I remember was a time I was on the Thai-Burma border and had just finished a hike. We stayed in the house of the village's first Christian. A missionary had been working there for sixty years. Two years before I stayed in this house, this missionary had converted the first person; it was a big deal. And I remember that night because the hike to get there took a while. We left at about ten o'clock at night and had to climb small mountains to get there. It was really late when we arrived, so we slept in the hut. I can still remember sleeping on the bamboo slotted floor. They had one modern piece of technology changing their world—a battery pack and a solar panel so they could listen to the radio. They pressed me, "Tell us what it's like where you are from."

How could I describe how different my way of life was from theirs? There are seasonal differences that are hard to describe, such as snow, but there are other, seemingly selfish, first-world differences that are difficult to explain. How could I describe a sleep-number bed to someone who slept on bamboo? When asked my favorite thing to drink, how could I explain a half cappuccino lite dry, while they were praying for clean water? How could I describe Disneyland to someone who had to walk three hours a day to get water? Language has limits.

The same is true, however, of my inability to express Uganda's beauty—how when I woke up in the morning, the color green was a deeper green than I had ever seen. How the light in people's eyes was brighter than the light I have ever seen in so many Americans' eyes. And how everyone I encountered has rhythm and can sing.

Everywhere I went, people sang! They even greeted me with song.

How could I describe the contrast of the bluest water, the greenest green, and the most orange clay I've ever seen along the road? How when the clouds opened and rain began to downpour, all I needed to do was grab a banana leaf and put it over my head. I don't have adequate language to describe how utterly beautiful Uganda is.

I believe this was the challenge John faced as he looked and saw a new heaven and a new earth. Maybe Paul said it right: "Eye has not seen, nor ear heard, nor have entered into the heart of man the things which God has prepared for those who love Him" (1 Corinthians 2:9 NKJV).

Believers won't be able to come close to describing what awaits those who belong to the Lamb. We won't be able to describe the infinite beauty of what awaits those who belong to the Lamb any differently than John was able to do.

The Revelation was given as a poetic, poimenic, prophetic work of art and vision to encourage, inspire, and let God's people know He stands with them in solidarity.

Perhaps you have been hanging onto the broken pieces of life that have been rattling around in your mind and soul. The grace of Jesus is what you need because you have been hanging on to something for too long and the broken pieces have been rattling around in your cage.

God has not forgotten those who are feeling the pain and pressure of life, and He has not forgotten His promises. May the Spirit breathe sweetly into your soul, "I am coming soon, bringing my reward with me to repay all people according to their deeds" (Revelation 22:12 NLT).

REFERENCES

Notes

1. Harris, Katherine. *Nelson's Foundational Bible Dictionary with the New King James Version Bible*. Thomas Nelson, 2014.

2. *The Oxford Handbook of Eschatology*. Edited by Jerry L. Walls. Oxford University Press, 2010, p. 12.

3. "The Roman Empire in the First Century: Titus & Domitian." *PBS*. http://www.pbs.org/empires/ romans/empire/titus_domitian.html.

4. Long, Phillip J. "The Roman Cult of Emperor Worship." *Reading Acts*. April 2, 2010. https://readingacts.com/2010/04/02/the-roman-cult-of-emperor-worship.

5. "Boiled in Oil but Remains Alive." *Voice of the Martyrs*. September 21, 2006. http://www.persecutionblog.com/2006/09/boiled_in_oil_b.html.

6. "Meaning of Numbers in the Bible: The Number 7." *The Bible Study Site*.

http://www.biblestudy.org/
bibleref/meaning-of-numbers-in-bible/7.html.

7. "Meaning of Numbers in the Bible: The Number 6." *The Bible Study Site.*
http://www.biblestudy.org/
bibleref/meaning-of-numbers-in-bible/6.html.

8. Zukeran, Patrick. "Four Views of Revelation." *Probe Ministries.* April 20, 2009.
https://www.probe.org/
four-views-of-revelation.

9. Warren, Mike. "Introduction to the Four Views." In *The Coming of Christ's Kingdom: The End Times and the Triumph of the Gospel.* Christian Civilization Publishing, 2010.
http://christianciv.com/
eschatology_bs_Sect1.htm.

10. Easton, Matthew George. "Entry for Martyr." "Easton's Bible Dictionary." *Bible Study Tools.*
http://www.biblestudytools.com/dictionaries/eastons-bible-dictionary/martyr.html.

11. "2347. thlipsis." *Strong's Greek Lexicon* (KJV). In *Blue Letter Bible.*
https://www.blueletterbible.org//
lang/lexicon/lexicon.cfm?Strongs=G2347&t=KJV.

12. "The Second Persecution, Under Domitian, A.D. 81." *Bible Study Tools.*
http://www.biblestudytools.com/
history/foxs-book-of-martyrs/the-second-persecution-under-domitian-a-d-81.html.

13. Keohane, Steve. "Sabbath Changed to Sunday." *Bible Probe.* http://www.bibleprobe.com/sundayworship.htm.

14. "How Did the Apostle John Die?" *The Bible Study Site.* http://www.biblestudy.org/question/how-did-apostle-john-die.html.

15. "991. blepo." From *Mounce Concise Greek-English Dictionary of the New* Testament, edited by William D. Mounce and Rick D. Bennett, Jr. https://gist.github.com/aaronshaf/7461620.

16. Wilkinson, Bruce and Kenneth Boa. *Talk Thru the Bible.* Thomas Nelson, 1983, pp. 221, 512.

17. "1577. ekklesia." From *NAS New Testament Greek Lexicon,* Thayer and Smith, 1999. http://www.biblestudytools.com/lexicons/greek/nas/ekklesia.html.

18. Billings, J. Todd. "The Problem with Incarnational Ministry." *Christianity Today.* August 10, 2012. http://www.christianitytoday.com/ct/2012/july-august/the-problem-with-incarnational-ministry.html.

19. Roberts, Mark D. "Ancient Ephesus and the New Testament." 2011. *Patheos.* http://www.patheos.com/blogs/markdroberts/series/ancient-ephesus-and-the-new-testament.

20. Padfield, David. "The City of Ephesus in Bible Times." *Bible Land History.* 2016.

http://www.biblelandhistory.com/turkey/
ephesus.html.

21. *Ibid.*

22. "Ephesus: The Jealousy of Jesus." May 24, 1998.
Discover the Book Ministries.
http://www.dtbm.org/
mcms_printpage.php?print=ephesus-the-
jealousy-of-jesus.

23. Watson, Donald L. "Domitian." *Ancient History
Encyclopedia.* April 25, 2013.
http://www.ancient.eu/
domitian.

24. "The Seven Cities of Revelation: Ephesus, First
Love." *Fishing the Abyss.*
http://www.fishingtheabyss.com/archives/302.

25. "The Assassination of Julius Caesar, 44 BC." *Eye
Witness to History.*
http://www.eyewitnesstohistory.com/caesar2.htm
.

26. Mark, Joshua J. "Augustus." *Ancient History
Encyclopedia.* 22 August 2010.
http://www.ancient.eu/
augustus.

27. "Tiberius Caesar." *Bible History Online.*
http://www.bible-history.com/sketches/
ancient/tiberius-caesar.html.

28. Franz, Gordon. "The Imperial Cult and the
Resurrection of the Lord Jesus." March 23, 2009.
Associates for Biblical Research.

http://www.biblearchaeology.org/post/2009/03/2
3/The-Imperial-Cult-and-the-Resurrection-of-the-
Lord-Jesus.aspx#Article.

29. "Nero." *History.* http://www.history.com/topics/
ancient-history/nero.

30. "History of the Roman Empire." *History World.*
http://www.historyworld.net/wrldhis/PlainTextHi
stories.asp?groupid=2730&HistoryID=ac58&gtra
ck=pthc

31. Wasson, Donald L. "Vespasian." *Ancient History
Encyclopedia.* 2012.
http://www.ancient.eu/Vespasian.

32. Wasson, Donald L. "Titus." *Ancient History
Encyclopedia.* 2013. http://www.ancient.eu/titus.

33. Wasson, Donald L. "Domitian." *Ancient History
Encyclopedia.* 2013.
http://www.ancient.eu/domitian.

34. Hirst, Kris K. "Old Smyrna (Turkey) Classical
Greek Site and Possible Home of Homer in
Anatolia." *ThoughtCo.* Updated March 8, 2018.
https://www.thoughtco.com/old-smyrna-turkey-
greek-site-172034.

35. "Bible Cities: Smyrna." *Bible History Online.*
http://www.bible-history.com/
links.php?cat=40&sub=688&cat_name=Bible+Ci
ties&subcat_name=Smyrna.

36. Glanville, Gary. "The Seven Churches of
Revelation (2) – Smyrna." February 6, 2011.
Romeo United Methodist Church.
http://www.romeoumc.com/templates/System/det
ails.asp?id=37949&PID=844793.

37. Santos, David Q. "The Seven Churches of Revelation: Introduction Part 1 of 8." September 12, 2009. *Biblical Connections.* http://biblicalconnections.blogspot.com/2009/09/seven-churches-of-revelation-david-q.html.

38. "2347. thlipis." From *Thayer's Greek Lexicon,* Biblesoft Inc., 2011. *Bible Hub.* http://biblehub.com/greek/2347.htm.

39. Carter, Joe. "5 Facts About Christian Persecution." October 30, 2015. *Action Institute.* http://blog.acton.org/archives/83011-5-facts-about-christian-persecution.html.

40. Tertullian. *Apologeticum (The Apology).* In *The Tertullian Project.* http://www.tertullian.org/works/apologeticum.htm.

41. Barclay, William. "Revelation 2:4." *William Barclay's Daily Study Bible.* In *StudyLight.org.* http://www.studylight.org/commentaries/dsb/view.cgi?bk=65&ch=2.

42. "The Message to Smyrna (Rev 2:8-11)." *Bible.org* https://bible.org/seriespage/4-message-smyrna-rev-28-11.

43. Graves, Dan. "#103 Polycarp's Martyrdom." From *The Martyrdom of Polycarp,* translated by J.B. Lightfoot, edited by Stephen Tomkins. *Christian History Institute.* https://www.christianhistoryinstitute.org/study/module/polycarp.

44. "Smyrna." From M.G. Easton, *Illustrated Bible Dictionary* (3rd ed.), Thomas Nelson, 1897. *Bible Study Tools.*

http://www.biblestudytools.com/dictionary/
smyrna.

45. "Gold, Frankincense, and Myrrh: The Gifts of the
    Wise Men (Magi)." December 15, 2013.
    Revelation.co.
    http://www.revelation.co/2013/12/15/gold-
    frankincense-and-myrrh-the-gifts-of-the-wise-
    men-magi.

46. "Myrrh." From M.G. Easton, *Illustrated Bible
    Dictionary* (3rd ed.), Thomas Nelson, 1897. *Bible
    Study Tools.*
    http://www.biblestudytools.com/dictionary/
    myrrh.

47. MacArthur, John. *GTY Newsletter.* May 15,
    2009. *Grace to You.* www.gty.org.

48. "Pergamum." *Encyclopaedia Britannica.*
    http://www.britannica.com/place/Pergamum.

49. Sansal, Burak. "Pergamum." *All About Turkey.*
    http://www.allaboutturkey.com/pergamum.htm.

50. Yeomans, Sarah. "Ancient Pergamon City of
    Science … and Satan?" December 15, 2016.
    Bible History Daily.
    http://www.biblicalarchaeology.org/
    daily/biblical-sites-places/biblical-archaeology-
    sites/pergamon-2.

51. Sansal, Burak. "Pergamum." *All About Turkey.*
    http://www.allaboutturkey.com/pergamum.htm.

52. Richison, Grant. "Revelation 2:13." October 19,
    1998. *Verse-by-Verse.*
    http://versebyversecommentary.com/revelation/re
    velation-213.

53. "Hebrews 9:4." From *John Gill's Exposition of the Bible*. *Bible Study Tools*. http://www.biblestudytools.com/commentaries/gills-exposition-of-the-bible/hebrews-9-4.html.

54. "Why Is God Going to Give Us a White Stone with a New Name?" *Got Questions*. https://www.gotquestions.org/white-stone-new-name.html.

55. Swindoll, Charles. *The Church Awakening: An Urgent Call for Renewal* (Reprint ed.). FaithWords, 2012.

56. Zacharias, Ravi. August 4, 2014. *Twitter*. https://twitter.com/ravizacharias/status/49631966 0413833216.

57. "Thyatira Weakness Made Strong." *God Rules*. http://www.godrules.net/library/ramsay/44ramsa y_a25.htm.

58. *Ibid*.

59. Astle, Cynthia. "How Jezebel Came to Be Known as a Wicked Queen." Updated March 8, 2017. *ThoughtCo*. http://ancienthistory.about.com/od/biowomen1/a/011311-CW-How-Jezebel-Came-To-Be-Known-As-The-Wicked-Queen-Jezebel.htm.

60. Alter, Alexandra. "Banned from Church." *Religion News Blog*. January 18, 2008. *Religion News Blog*. http://www.religionnewsblog.com/20385/shunning.

61. "Biblical Sites in Turkey – Sardis." *Biblical Tour Guide.* http://www.biblicaltourguide.com/sardissardessard.html.

62. *Ibid.*

63. Jastrow, Morris. "Breastplate of the High Priest." *Jewish Encyclopedia.* http://www.jewishencyclopedia.com/articles/366 8-breastplate-of-the-high-priest.

64. "Sardis City of the Dead Church." *Bible Charts.* http://www.biblecharts.org/biblelandnotes/Sardis. pdf.

65. "The Letter to the Church at Sardis." *Redland Baptist Church.* http://www.redlandbaptist.org/sermon/the-letter-to-the-church-at-sardis.

66. "The Letters to the 7 Churches of Asia: Philadelphia." *Truth for Today.* http://www.biblecourses.com/english/en_lessons/en_198912_10.pdf54.

67. "Philadelphia – The Seven Churches of Revelation." *The Bible Study Site.* http://www.biblestudy.org/biblepic/churches-of-revelation-philadelphia.html.

68. *Ibid.*

69. *Ibid.*

70. Phillips, Ron. "7 Demons That Attack the Church." *Charisma Magazine.* July 5, 2013. http://www.charismamag.com/spirit/spiritual-warfare/11355-seven-demons-that-attack-the-church1.

71. "40. hagios." From *Thayer's Greek Lexicon*, 2011, Biblesoft, Inc. *Bible Hub.* http://biblehub.com/ greek/40.htm.

72. "228. aléthinos." From *Thayer's Greek Lexicon*, 2011, Biblesoft, Inc. *Bible Hub.* http://biblehub.com/str/greek/228.htm.

73. Guptill, Denn. "A Tale of Seven Churches: Laodicea." April 14, 2003. *Sermon Central.* http://www.sermoncentral.com/sermons/a-tale-of-seven-churches-laodicea-denn-guptill-sermon-on-book-of-revelation-57182.asp.

74. Ritenbaugh, John W. "The World, the Church, and Laodiceanism." *Bible Tools.* 1993. http://www.bibletools.org/index.cfm/fuseaction/Library.sr/CT/CGGBOOKLETS/k/452/World-Church-Laodiceanism.htm.

75. "Revelation Chapter Three – Laodicea." *Apostle.org.* http://www.apostle.org/lectures/rev3lao.htm.

76. *Ibid.*

77. *Ibid.*

78. "281. amen." *Strong's Greek Lexicon* (KJV). In *Blue Letter Bible.* https://www.blueletterbible.org//lang/lexicon/lexicon.cfm?Strongs=G281&t=KJV.

79. Ritenbaugh, John W. "The World, the Church, and Laodiceanism." *Bible Tools.* 1993.

80. Page, Helen. "Hierapolis – A Sacred City Built on Thermal Springs." *Travel Sign Posts.*

http://www.travelsignposts.com/Turkey/destinati ons/hierapolis.

81. Viereck, George Sylvester. *Glimpses of the Great.* Macauley, 1930.

82. Roberts, Mark D. "Thin Places: A Biblical Investigation." 2012. *Patheos.* http://www.patheos.com/ blogs/markdroberts/series/thin-places.

83. Amos, Jonathan. "Astronomers Detect 'Monster Star.'" July 21, 2010. *BBC.* http://www.bbc.co.uk/ news/science-environment-10707416.

84. Connor, Steve. "The Star That's Ten Million Brighter Than the Sun." *Independent.* http://www.independent.co.uk/news/science/the-star-thats-ten-million-times-brighter-than-the-sun-2032215.html.

85. Einstein, Albert. *Living Philosophies.* Simon and Schuster, 1931.

86. Foster, Richard. *Celebration of Discipline: The Path to Spiritual Growth.* Harper, 1988.

87. Peterson, Eugene. *Living the Message.* Harper, 1996.

88. "Manners and Customs: Seals." *Bible History Online.* http://www.bible-history.com/ links.php?cat=39&sub=467&cat_name=Manners +%26+Customs&subcat_name=Seals.

89. "4969. sphazō." *Strong's Greek Lexicon* (KJV). In *Blue Letter Bible.*

https://www.blueletterbible.org/
lang/lexicon/lexicon.cfm?Strongs=G4969&t=KJ
V.

90. "What Is the Biblical Significance of the Number
    Seven/7?" *Got Questions Ministries.*
    https://www.gotquestions.org/number-7-
    seven.html.

91. "2521. kathémai." From *Strong's Greek Lexicon*
    (KJV). *Bible Hub.* https://biblehub.com/greek/
    strongs_2521.htm.

92. Sittser, Jeremy. *A Grace Disguised: How the
    Souls Grows Through Loss.* Zondervan, 2009.

93. "The Romans Destroy the Temple at Jerusalem,
    70 AD." *Eyewitness to History.*
    http://www.eyewitnesstohistory.com/jewishtempl
    e.htm.

94. "Triumph Ancient Roman Honour."
    Encyclopedia Britannia.
    http://www.britannica.com/topic/triumph-
    ancient-Roman-honour.

95. Brown, John Pairman. *Israel and Hellas: Sacred
    Institutions with Roman Counterparts.* De
    Gruyter, 2002.

96. "5515. cloros." From *Thayer's Greek Lexicon,*
    2011, Biblesoft, Inc. *Bible Hub.*
    http://biblehub.com/greek/
    5515.htm.

97. Chilver, Guy Edward Farquhar. "Domitian
    Roman Emperor." *Encyclopedia Britannica.*
    http://www.britannica.com/biography/Domitian.

98. Rawlings, Matt. "How to Read the Book of Revelation for All Its [sic] Worth." July 25, 2016. *Pastor Matt's Blog.* http://www.pastormattsblog.com/blog/how-to-read-the-book-of-revelation-for-all-its-worth.

99. Guzik, David. "Revelation 6 – The First Six Seals." *Enduring Word.* 2013. https://enduringword.com/commentary/revelation-6/

100. Guzik, David. "Revelation 8 – The First Four Trumpets." *Enduring Word.* 2013. https://enduringword.com/commentary/revelation-8/

101. "Significance of the Shofar the Shout of God's Victory." *Hebrew for Christians.* http://www.hebrew4christians.com/Holidays/Fall_Holidays/Elul/Shofar/shofar.html.

102. "894. apsinthion." *Strong's Greek Lexicon* (KJV). In *Blue Letter Bible.* https://www.blueletterbible.org/lang/lexicon/lexicon.cfm?Strongs=G894&t=KJV.

103. "12. abyssos." *Strong's Greek Lexicon* (KJV). In *Blue Letter Bible.* https://www.blueletterbible.org/lang/lexicon/lexicon.cfm?Strongs=G12&t=KJ.

104. Croley, Wayne. "The Difference Between Fallen Angels and Demons." *Prophecy Proof Insights.*

http://www.prophecyproof.org/2010/10/underst
anding-the-enemy-the-difference-between-
fallen-angels-and-demons.

105. Ralby, Aaron. "Roman-Parthian War, 55—36
BCE: The Beginnings of War." *Atlas of
Military History*. Parragon, 2013, 66–67.

106. Di Pietro, JJ. "Smith Wigglesworth." *Cane
Creek Church*.
http://canecreekchurch.org/what-s-your-
legacy/44-smith-wigglesworth.

107. Einstein, Albert. *Living Philosophies*. Simon
and Shuster, 1931.

108. "975. biblion." From *Englishman's
Concordance*. *Bible Hub*.
http://biblehub.com/greek/975.htm.

109. "974. biblaridion." From *Thayer's Greek
Lexicon*, 2011, Biblesoft, Inc. *Bible Hub*.
http://biblehub.com/greek/974.htm.

110. Lewis, Steve. "Theological Presuppositions and
the Interpretation of Revelation." *Conservative
Theological Journal* (August 2003). In *Spirit
and Truth*.
http://www.spiritandtruth.org/teaching/docume
nts/articles/5/5.htm?x=x#sdfootnote8sym.

111. "3144. martys." *Strong's Greek Lexicon* (ESV).
In *Blue Letter Bible*.
https://www.blueletterbible.org/
lang/lexicon/lexicon.cfm?Strongs=G3144&t=E
SV.

112. "Who Is Satan? Who Is the Devil?" *Got Questions Ministries.*
https://www.gotquestions.org/who-Satan.html.

113. "What Is the Significance of a Scarlet Thread?" *Got Questions Ministries.*
https://www.gotquestions.org/
scarlet-thread.html.

114. Ross, Allen. "The Slaughter of the Innocents (Matthew 2:13-23)." March 15, 2006.
Bible.org. https://bible.org/seriespage/4-slaughter-innocents-matthew-213-23.

115. Walvoord, John. "The Rise and Fall of Babylon." January 1, 2008. *Bible.org.*
https://bible.org/
seriespage/5-rise-and-fall-babylon.

116. "Jews in Roman Times." From *The Roman Empire in the First Century AD. PBS.*
http://www.pbs.org/
empires/romans/empire/jews.html.

117. "Phylactery." *Encyclopedia Britannica.*
http://www.britannica.com/topic/phylactery.

118. "Hebrew Gematria." *Hebrew for Christians.*
http://www.hebrew4christians.com/Grammar/U
nit_Eight/Hebrew_Gematria/hebrew_gematria.h
tml.

119. Anthony, Richard. "The Mark of the Beast." *Ecclesia.org.*
http://www.ecclesia.org/truth/beast.html.

120. "What Is the Great White Throne Judgment?" *Got Questions Ministries.*

https://www.gotquestions.org/
great-white-throne-judgment.html.

121. Van der Hoeven, Jan Willem. "Armageddon: In
the Valley of Jezreel, or Jehoshaphat?" *Israel
My Beloved.*
http://israelmybeloved.com/armageddon-in-the-
valley-of-jezreel-or-jehoshaphat.

122. Sissom, Carolyn. "The Song of Moses II – Rev
15." *Eastgate Ministries.* March 7, 2010.
http://www.eastgateministries.com/index.php?o
ption=com_content&task=view&id=346&Itemi
d=66.

123. "The Song of Moses, and the Song of the
Lamb." *Judeo-Christian Research.* 2001.
http://juchre.org/articles/song.htm.

124. Mason, Mike. *The Gospel According to Job.*
Crossway, 1994.

125. Rayburn, Dusty. "The Names of God: Moshia',
My Deliverer." October 25, 2010. *Devoted
Conversations.*
https://www.devotedconversations.com/the-
names-of-god-moshia-my-deliverer.

126. Parker, Theodore. *Ten Sermons of Religion* of
Justice and the Conscience. Crosby, Nichols
and Company, 1853, pp. 84–85.

127. Yancey, Philip. *The Jesus I Never Knew.*
Zondervan, 2002.

128. "4057. midbar." *Strong's Hebrew Lexicon*
(KJV). In *Blue Letter Bible.*
https://www.blueletterbible.org/
lang/lexicon/lexicon.cfm?t=kjv&strongs=h4057

129. Phillips, Jenny. "Jesus and Wilderness." *American Bible Society.* http://bibleresources.americanbible.org/resource /jesus-and-wilderness.

130. Guzik, David. "Revelation 17 – The Fall of Religious Babylon." *Enduring Word.* https://enduringword.com/commentary/revelati on-17.

131. Lewis, C. S. *Reflections on the Psalms.* Mariner Books, 1964.

132. Nouwen, Henri J. M. *In the Name of Jesus.* Crossroad, 1992.

133. Tozer, A. W. *Preparing for Jesus' Return Daily Live the Blessed Hope.* Bethany House, 2012.

134. Kay, Glenn. "Jewish Wedding Customs and the Bride of Messiah." *Grafted-In Ministries.* http://messianicfellowship.50webs.com/weddin g.html.

135. Smith, William. "Entry for 'Number.'" *Smith's Bible Dictionary*, 1901. In *Bible Study Tools.* http://www.biblestudytools.com/dictionary/num ber.

136. "What Is Dispensationalism?" *Global Christian Center.* http://globalchristiancenter.com/bible- and-theology/systematic-theology/24553-what- is-dispensationalism.

137. "The Doctrine of Rewards: The Judgment Seat (Bema) of Christ." *Bible.org.* https://bible.org/article/ doctrine-rewards-judgment-seat-bema-christ.

138. Alcorn, Randy. *50 Days of Heaven: Reflections That Bring Eternity to Light.* Tyndale, 2006.

139. Lewis, C. S. *The Last Battle.* Macmillan, 1956.

140. Jobs, Steven. "Steve Jobs' 2005 Stanford Commencement Address." *Stanford News.* http://news.stanford.edu/2005/06/14/jobs-061505.

About the Author

Monty C. Wright, PhD, is a husband, dad, speaker, teacher, writer, activist, and pastor who has an insatiable love of learning. He is the President of Planet Changer, an international non-profit organization; the founder of the Bible Institute of Seattle, author of the book *Sacred Space* and the leadership program The Timothy Institute. Monty is also the founder and lead pastor of Snoqualmie Valley Alliance Church. Currently, he resides in Fall City, Washington, with his amazing wife, Amy.

About Sermon To Book

SermonToBook.com began with a simple belief: that sermons should be touching lives, *not* collecting dust. That's why we turn sermons into high-quality books that are accessible to people all over the globe.

Turning your sermon series into a book exposes more people to God's Word, better equips you for counseling, accelerates future sermon prep, adds credibility to your ministry, and even helps make ends meet during tight times.

John 21:25 tells us that the world itself couldn't contain the books that would be written about the work of Jesus Christ. Our mission is to try anyway. Because in heaven, there will no longer be a need for sermons or books. Our time is now.

If God so leads you, we'd love to work with you on your sermon or sermon series.

Visit www.sermontobook.com to learn more.

48152984R00212

Made in the USA
Columbia, SC
06 January 2019